Tyler's Pain

JANETTE RUFFIN-RUSHER

iUniverse, Inc.
New York Bloomington

Tyler's Pain

iUniverse books may be ordered through booksellers or by contacting:

iUniverse
1663 Liberty Drive
Bloomington, IN 47403
www.iuniverse.com
1-800-Authors (1-800-288-4677)

Because of the dynamic nature of the Internet, any Web addresses or links contained in this book may have changed since publication and may no longer be valid. The views expressed in this work are solely those of the author and do not necessarily reflect the views of the publisher, and the publisher hereby disclaims any responsibility for them.

ISBN: 978-1-4502-6137-1 (sc)
ISBN: 978-1-4502-6135-7 (ebook)
ISBN: 978-1-4502-6136-4 (dj)

Library of Congress Control Number: 2010914027

Printed in the United States of America

iUniverse rev. date: 10/06/2010

I F ANYONE WOULD HAVE TOLD ME 20 years ago that I would be living in a small community that did not necessary embrace African Americans, I would have said yeah right. Let's see where do I begin, new job, new apartment, not bad for just the Summer of 2002. I am a single mom and work as a Account Specialist for an Electronics Company. Tyler my daughter who is 10 yrs old, was pretty excited considering all summer every day the apartment swimming pool was a great new toy for her. Oh yeah I enjoyed it also. All summer Tyler and I shopped for clothes for back to school. "Mommy this is so cool getting regular clothes instead uniforms."

I always loved the way Tyler had such a great attitude about school, she was the type of child would rather go to the library then the toy store a great deal of the time.

So that first day of school we were both in such great spirits, just looking forward to new friends, cool teachers and just fun. Tyler and I got to the school orientation early; just enough to get a great seat close to the front for the speakers and the teacher to be introduced. I remember the principal was a tall middle age woman with light hair and according to her credentials was very well qualified. She seemed very much interested in any and all questions. I decided to ask about if children carried their own inhalers with a doctor's permission slip would it be allowed. The principal I remember smiled and responded "Oh yes madam, of course with a doctors slip on file." "Thank you," I replied. Tyler looked up at me and smiled, with that assurance and friendly reply from the principal, we looked over the fact that we were the only black family in the orientation. I certainly was not prejudiced and did not raise Tyler to be. Don't get me wrong, I knew of this city's history, it was not exactly great with African Americans, but I felt that everywhere in this country there would be intelligent people as well as ignorant ones. The approach here was purely positive.

1

Tyler was so excited not knowing what to wear. I remember her saying this is so cool mom, no uniforms I can accessorize her favorite word. My daughter was tall for her age, but in my eyes she was always my little girl. I remember purposely waiting after she turned 5 being that her birthday was in December, so as to have another whole year to enjoy her as much as possible. "Mommy this is so cool. Just like the shows I watch on the Disney channel I will have friends of different races. Mommy I can't wait to tell you about my first day!" Tyler always had no problem making friends with anyone. I loved the fact I had raised her to be a loving child. It was always fun to play house, o yeah I am a Barbie fanatic. As my daughter sometimes put it mommy you are such a girlie girl. Tyler would be fine. Tyler was so excited her first day, new outfit and all.

The drive to work was not necessary different, If anything a little faster. My mind was on her first day, and how excited she would be once she got home to tell me about it. Late August was so beautiful, still leaves on trees and such a warm right day. I looked forward to my half hour lunches considering I spent them outside usually sitting in my car, enjoying the sunshine. Two months on the job there was still a lot to learn, selling electronic parts was not an easy job. Work environment was actually quite nice, many of the new employees much like myself had all come from the same cellular company thru layoff like me. So of course I had several friends. Karry and I had met 3 years prior at the cellular company and became fast friends, it didn't matter that she was white and I black. We had similar interests she assisted in my training in the Finance Department at the previous job, I sat next to her and we shared stories about each having a son and feeling blessed. I noticed that Karry had a bible out on her desk and I commented that I too tried to always have time to read the Bible while at work. That set the stage for us to because good friends. A year later I received a promotion to another department, but we always found time to say hello while passing each other.

Karry was actually the reason I had picked the apartment. Karry lived also in this little suburb not far from the job, and suggested it. I mentioned that I wanted to be close to work, because of Tyler's asthma in case of emergency. After looking over the apartment together, Karry and I, I fell in love with it. The building was very nice, close to work actually a 20 minute drive. So it was perfect. "Karry, doesn't this city have a reputation for not exactly being crazy about African Americans moving here?" "Oh Janette, things have changed haven't you noticed this is a mixed building of all different nationalities. It's a bargain you should take it!"

I was not quite prepared for I received once I got home. Upon entering the apartment I expected Tyler to greet me......"Tyler, Tyler..!" I watched anxiously as Tyler approached me slowly while hearing her crieds steady amerge louder "mommy this girl Amber kicked dirt on me and called me nigger and blacky. The other kids did not want to play with me, all I wanted was some shade mommy I was standing under a tree in the playground" As she looked into my eyes for some type of shelter..over me came the sad feeling that I had failed my daughter I reached out to hug my Tyler hoping somehow I could remove her hurt into my body..unfortunately I only felt more helplessness with each tremble and shake of her body crying against mine.

As I sat Tyler down that night I remember telling Tyler that there are some ignorant people in this world and unfortunately we sometimes have to come across them. Tyler and I had discussed racism before, but she had never experienced it first hand. I searched for the words to explain that she should go to the school with a positive attitude and not let a one ignorant child stop her from learning. I asked Tyler had she spoken to the teacher to which she replied "yes mommy, I told the teacher right after we went to class after the recess," "well what did she say?" looking concerned to Tyler. "She called her to the front of the class and Amber denied that she had called me a name". "Tyler what did the teacher do at that point?" "Mommy she looked as if she did not believe me and said Tyler have a seat, Amber says that nothing was said so have a seat."

At dinner that night I told Tyler I was going to call the school and send a note to her teacher to call me. Secretly I didn't want to believe this was happening to us. Had I made a decision without truly examining all the factors here? This was a middle class neighborhood, yes predominately white on the west side of Cleveland but I loved our new home. I was not a prejudiced person and was not going to let one incident ruined my child and my happiness about our new apartment and job. As I watched over Tyler sleep that night I wondered had I failed as a parent, although I had spoke to Tyler about prejudice in the past nothing can prepare a parent for a child to be directly affected or touched.

Was I so consumed with getting the new apartment, new job, doing it on my own that I didn't closely examine the situation I put my daughter in? Hey I thought I am over analyzing this, after all there was bound to be some ignorant kids as well as adults we both would encounter.

Tyler and I would talk in the morning I would tell her to be strong .I would console her I thought. I wasn't going to let this happy time for us fade. I couldn't let my family know what was going on at least not yet . I could see my mother now "I don't know what you were thinking going to the west side of Cleveland anyway, and of all places Parma!" My mother is from the south, and in her seventies along with my father. I remember my dad saying the word colored back when I was a child. My dad before he retired was a truck driver and always had friends of all races. We were not taught to be racist. As a matter of fact at his retirement party ninety percent of the guests there, were of different nationalities friends of my father, from work and their families. The other ten percent made up family and friends it was just an out pouring of love. However in Cleveland the majority of blacks live on the east side of Cleveland, and the whites the west side.

I got Tyler up extra early since I had to be at work at 9. I needed to drop her off at the early morning childcare at the school. This was a great program I thought considering the school that Tyler attended provided the program and I could just feel secure she got to school safe and was on time. Tyler mainly nodded her head while I spoke to her about giving the teacher the note. "Mommy I'm sorry I was not strong yesterday...I will avoid the bad kids and just be a good girl." Tears welled up in her eyes as she looked at me searching for some answer to still her. "Tyler didn't I tell you that God sees everything?" "Yes mommy". "Well he also knows your heart and knows you are a good child and will keep you safe. Baby pray the 23rd psalm to yourself Tyler. It will be okay, I know how strong you are mommy loves you." At that moment Tyler gave me the largest and tightest hung, I could feel she did not want to let me go.

As I walked Tyler into the large gym that the before school program was held in, it was apparent that Tyler was definitely the minority here. I saw only one other young black child. As

I signed Tyler in I noticed silent polite stares, from the child care workers. "Good morning!" I thought breaking the silent, would at least get a response." "Good morning how are you!" "Fine thank you, you ladies have a nice day!" As Tyler hung up her book bag a couple of girls came over to ask her to play Barbie with them. I smiled as I saw Tyler smile and look at me. I told her I love you Tyler and kissed her hurriedly as she rushed to play.

It was great that I worked fairly close to my home. I felt that the move to be close to home was great considering Tyler had asthma and if she had a serious problem at school I would be able to get to her faster. Going in to this new job had its own set of challenges. I never sold electronic parts before, but I had great people skills and felt I was up for it.

The 4 weeks of training was intense mainly classroom and direct live calls in the last week. Being in my own little cubicle at this point I knew if Tyler needed to call for any reason she could reach me without any problems. My thoughts were steadily on her while I seemed to be in auto pilot for placing the headset over my head along with signing in to my computer. I wondered how her day was going, and if she had made any new friends Tyler never had a problem making friends, she would do fine I hoped.

During lunch I took the time to call her school and was unable to get the principal only able to leave a message. I remember calling back several times to no avail with the same response of "she is not available would you like to leave a message." I decided to think positive and hope Tyler was having a better day. I got off at 5 o'clock and needed to pick Tyler up by 6:00, good thing the drive to the school was no more than 30 minutes considering rush hour traffic and all. Upon picking Tyler up from school she was very distressed she had a small envelope in her hand, there was one childcare worker left for the remaining students. I should have known something was wrong because as I signed Tyler out of the childcare on the roll sheet the childcare worker avoided eye contact purposely. I tried to ask Tyler what was wrong, just by the look on her face. Tyler only responded with her head down "I will tell you in the car mommy". As she picked up her book bag and we walked to the car. I felt the adrenaline immediately build wondering was next! I had not noticed before but as we got into the car the envelope Tyler handed to me held her beads that I had put into her hair. Tyler started to cry at this point "mommy this little girl had her hands in my hair while I was on the jungle jim and would not let go, I screamed for her to let go but she would not mommy". As I pulled into the parking lot I wondered still was this for real? "Tyler I don't understand why did she have her hands in your hair from the start anyway?" "Mommy she wanted to know how the beads were put in my braids and how they come out so she pulled really hard and it hurt and pulled them out!" By this time we had walked to the apartment building and we were at the elevators. I decided to just go to the apartment and finish the conversation there. Suddenly the lovely apartment I could not wait to get looked not so lovely. Once inside I found out Tyler had a red spot around her roots where I had place the beads when I did her hair. What was even more interesting was the fact that Tyler said the childcare workers did nothing but tell the child to apologize and give the beads to another black child to place them back. As if oh! she had to know how she is black, so she can place them back. I did not know what to think! That night Tyler and I talked about a lot of things, we made dinner together and I assured Tyler I would speak to the childcare staff the next morning. The last thing I needed was to show Tyler I felt quite angry, and along with no messages returned on my cell or the home voicemail from the school I was not so HAPPY.

Tyler came to me the next morning while getting ready for school and asked, "why do you think some people are just mean mom?" "Well Tyler, I just don't know I guess the question could also be why are some people nice?" "Only god knows mommy, or like you say sometimes how people are raised?" With that I nodded my head. Tyler looked at me as if she knew in my mind I also had more questions. It is the look children give parents when we know they are aware we are puzzled too. I prayed a silent prayer as Tyler and I walked down the hall to the elevator. All I wanted to do was to resolve the situation right away. Being that it was only the first week of school I took into consideration the fact that there was probably a lot of parents calling about supplies, books, classes and other important matters. Not to overshadow the fact that I was still awaiting an acknowledgement of my messages and still a lot peeved about my daughter's hair.

Tyler had seen me be quite firm when it came to getting my point across. I believe I am like any other parent who loves their child, we just want our child to be treated fairly. When we arrived at the school childcare program this morning, I walked in thinking what could the possible answer I was going to get regarding the hair incident. "Good morning who would I speak to regarding a situation that occurred yesterday with my daughter's hair?" A short middle aged woman spoke up with blonde hair. "How can I help you?" After explaining the playground incident from the day before, I was quite surprised to hear "oh the kids were just playing." To this I replied while showing the redness in Tyler's head where the braid was "how do you play where one child wants another to stop pulling her braid and it ends in crying and pain?" At this point the other ladies looked as if I was making a big deal out of nothing. The last thing I wanted was to have my daughter viewed as the trouble maker kid. The short blonde haired older woman spoke up to say, "The parent of the child involved was notified and the child also apologized, this will not happen again." "I should hope not because that is definitely not the way children should play!" I remember at this point the ladies had nothing more to say. There was silence which seemed odd..but then I broke in with "You ladies have a nice day!!" I then kissed Tyler who looked at me with that I guess you told them mommy. Actually nothing could of have been more from the truth. The silence felt that morning was only a validation that there was more silence to come.

My drive to work seemed so quick that morning maybe because I was mainly thinking about my daughter and the reaction of the childcare teachers. While signing in to my computer that morning Karry came by to say hello. "How is it going Janette, you catching on to these electronic parts girlfriend?" "Hey I can only give it my best shot, this is a thick catalog you know." "Lunch today Janette?" "Sure see you at 12:30." With that Karry retreated to her cubicle on the other side of the floor. It had because a ritual with us so far we had lunch either sitting in her car or mine or just talked together in the lunchroom. Lunch was just 30 minutes and went fast but great to have a friend, especially now.

My day was cut out for me. Very busy none stop, at one point I felt I was never going to get this capacitor stuff, I mean when you say electronic to me, I thought of spark plugs in the past. By lunch my head was swimming I think I must have taken over 50 calls, seemed not a lot but with calls sometimes taking more than 5 mins, because of assisting customers with additional parts and supplies. Which of course I was still learning it was quite challenging. In my cubicle I had charts of every sort, diagrams, suggestive selling tools for items to sell, any and everything to help me. Can't say I was not determined.

I was thankful just to have a job. I mean how many people go thru a layoff and shortly thereafter find a new job. I felt blessed.

Lunchtime came not soon enough. Karry arrived right on time.. we had a system that we would email each other at least 5 mins before lunch. This would make sure the other person was wrapping up their task. "Hey Janette, where's lunch at today?" As I removed my purse from the desk drawer, all I could think of was my daughter Tyler and how was her day going. "Oh I don't know, let's go to McDonalds." "Cool Janette!" Even though I wanted to take the elevator, today was a day I had no problems taking the stairs. Although it was in the fall the weather was still very nice. A little warm, but not quite fall weather. While approaching the cars in the parking lot Karry asked, "how is Tyler doing in school." To this I replied "well let's see, first I have been sending notes to school with Tyler every day, with no response, along with calling the school with no luck with my messages." "What exactly is happening?" "Where do I begin, Tyler is having a lot of problems at her new school. What type of problems I don't want to say prejudice, but it is just that. I am beginning to feel that I should have not moved over here to Parma, because I don't want to feel that this is happening to my child." "Well Janette don't you feel that you are over reacting to this whole thing, I mean couldn't it just be a thing that Tyler is just not used to her new school and enviroment and wants you to stay home with her?" "I really don't think so Karry. For example today I had to go to the school childcare before school to address a situation about hair pulling, this child wanted to see how it was to have beads in Tyler's hair and how it was connected!?" "Wait a minute slow down explain to me what you are talking about" "Tyler was on the playground jungle jim, you know that thing kids climb on and this little girl decides to latch on to one of Tyler's beads to see how it was connected. Tyler asked her to let go and she didn't meanwhile all along pulling her hair as hard as she could" "Oh my god so what happen?" "Tyler screamed for the girl to stop the teachers came over, but not until blood was draw in her scalp!" "I feel awful Janette, but don't you feel that maybe this was an isolated incident and there is no prejudice or malice their just kids playing?" "Karry they were not playing Tyler did not even know this kid." "Well the bottom line she is okay know right?" "Yeah Karry, but that is not the point, you seem to think that old slogan kids will be kids applies here." "You know Janette we are going to be late for work, I think it is time to head back, see you at break right," "Sure Karry." With that we both headed back in to the office and parted. On the way back I could not help but feel that Karry thought I was making a big deal out of nothing, which I certainly did not feel that way.

As I hurried back to the office and my cubicle, I placed my headset on praying a silent prayer, hoping Tyler's day was going to be okay.

It been a busy afternoon on phones all day, never in my wildest dreams did I think I would be selling capacitors and resistors, I think I do real well sounding as if I know what exactly they do. I mean the job is exciting in the fact that there is something to learn new each day. Although I did not have an electronics degree, I had great people skills and could talk to anyone and understood how to research and find out information on anything in electronics I needed to.

Newark Electronics was a great place to work, from what I could see, and tell and if you did not mind being on the phone all day and taking calls and processing orders, I did not have a problem with it. I mean my last position I was use to heavy call volume and it was a challenge if anything.

Whew the afternoon has been hectic none stop, while working around 3:30pm, Karry I notice had emailed me according to the little icon on the bottom of my computer ready for break I read? I responded with no I think I will just sit at my desk today. She responded with an email of "what's wrong are you made at me?" "Of course not I'm just going to sit at my desk, okay talk to you later". With that I sent the email reply back and just sat there. I sure hope traffic was not so backed up today after I got off at 5:00 because even though I just worked 20 min from home; my route went directly under several freeway entrances and exits. I was cutting it quite close to 6:00 o'clock the deadline for kids to be picked up in the afternoon program.

I guess it never dawned on me that being that I was in a commercial area "Janette your are not the only person getting off at 5:00pm!" Sometimes it seemed as if I was sitting in traffic for 30mins just to get close to my apartment. What ever happened to the 30 min drive or 20 min drive, I don't know it seemed as if everyone was in my way from now on. Finally. I pulled into the school lot at 5:57pm I felt so defeated no extra time. As I walked into the gym I hear so loudly my feet echo on the hard wood floors. "I am so sorry I am late traffic". The last attendant just smiled I could hear another mother coming behind me.

Tyler was playing with some other little girl kicking a ball around the gym. "Tyler get your coat lets go, get your book bag." "Mommy I missed you today," "I missed you too, how was your day?" "Let just go home mommy." We walked to the car outside hand in hand. Times like this I often thought of when Tyler first went to school in kindergarten and she held my hand so tight to assure she was going to be okay. "So Tyler how was your day?" "Mommy lets talk at home okay". Driving home I wondered what was up now with Tyler, the drive was short but silent.

As we entered the apartment I could only guess what was up next. My routine with Ty was to have her take her school books to her room and start her homework, while I got undressed and prepared dinner. Ty usually always wanted to help me in the kitchen, so I was a bit concerned when she shut her door and did not come right out. "Ty Ty what's up don't you want to help with dinner?" I knocked on her bedroom door and heard her russle some papers as I preceded to open her room door. "Mommy I would like to just start my homework now okay." Ty's head lowered to her books in front of her, .. "Okay Ty no problem I will just start dinner and I think it is a great idea since you are so focused right now, just be sure to hang up your school clothes okay?" She nodded, which was strange since I knew my daughter so well she always had something to say even if it was just a low okay or yeah. I slowly closed the door and walked back to my bedroom to look out the window in my room. My apartment faced toward the back of the building. From the sixth floor I glazed out to the street below watching the cars and people, although I looked out into the view I could only see my daughter's face wondering what was on her mind.

"Mommy I smell the food in the kitchen, what's for dinner?' As I turned around I could see Ty was there, "Honey you remember that meatloaf I made last night and placed in the fridge, well that's it!" "Cool what else?" "Hey how about some vegetables you love corn huh?'

Yeah mommy, I will go and wash up okay? Tyler abruptly went down the hall to the washroom, except it was as if she could not wait to change the conversation and just quickly get to where I could not see her face clearly. Sometimes a mother just knows that there is something wrong, but not sure as to what. I could feel it but was almost afraid to ask, she seemed distant but on the surface kinda cheery, I wondered if I over thinking this or what.

As I set the table, Tyler entered the kitchen and got the juice out of the refrigerator . "Mommy I'm done with my homework so if you would like to check it I could bring it to you" "Thanks sweetie, I'll check it after dinner okay so Tyler how was school today?" I looked across the table at Ty and she was just stirring her food around in her plate. The feeling in the kitchen was tense although it was just myself and Tyler. Tyler slowly looked up at me and signed. ."Mommy I know we just moved here and it is a nice apartment mommy I appreciate everything, and don't want to complain or anything" "Tyler stop right there, I love you very much and you are very important to me. I would not ever take what you say lightly, hey aren't you my angel?" "Yes mommy," "So you know what ever you say I want to listen to. Hey tell me did you make any new friends today?" "One little girl name Heather, wants to be my friend she is so nice mommy, I sat with her at lunch. Mommy she has blonde hair like my Barbie doll and she spikes it too. It is so cool she lets me sit with her at lunch." Suddenly Tyler's voice trailed off and got low..I could see the sadness came over her and her head lowered. "Ty what is it.. tell me." "Mommy when I was in the lunch room today in line a tall girl said to me you don't belong here people like you need to go back to their side of town. Mommy she pointed her finger at me in my face in the lunch line I was so ashamed and feel scared, I just got my food and went to try and find a seat that's when Heather said you can sit here." "Tyler had you seen this girl before, that confronted you today?" "No mommy, she was taller than me and I did not say anything to her, just got my food as fast as I could and went to find a seat. That's when Heather saw me upset with my tray and asked me to sit with her." It hurt to see Tyler begin to cry, at that moment I felt helpless and confused, didn't I realize that kids could be cruel, especially prejudice ones. "Tyler don't cry it will be okay, if it makes you feel better I will go to school with you and speak to the principal about this incident so as to nip it in the bud, okay." "Mommy what about your job won't you be late?" "No Ty I will leave a voice mail on my supervisors phone to let them know I will be maybe a little late, it will be okay baby, just finish your dinner, Tyler it is unfortunate that you have to encounter some kids that are mean, I just want you to remember that all people are not that way." "Like your friend Karry," "Yeah exactly like that, she and I have known each other for over 3yrs and she is white and very nice. Haven't I told you that ignorance comes in all races, both black and white?" "Yes mommy you do." "So Tyler finish your dinner and let's not let one stupid little girl spoil our dinner okay angel?" "Okay mommy" We finished dinner in silent, why did I feel while we occasionally looked up at each other during dinner, Ty seem to let this stew on her brain and wanted to say more.

That night while Tyler slept I checked over her homework, while doing so I questioned in my mind what was I doing to Tyler inside. Sure everything wasn't terrible, I had a great new apartment in a racially mixed building. There was even a nice old white lady down the hall, whom although I did not know her name as she passed my apartment she spoke with me and Ty when ever she saw us. I wanted to keep an open mind about what was going on here. Yes this was a big adjustment but I did not want to believe that this would escalate to anything more. I wanted to chalk this up as just Tyler meeting a few jerks and over all it was going to be okay. Watching Tyler sleep I thought of how much I loved her and wanted the best for her. Memories of the first day of school came to mind, as well as how excited she was to as she put it "go to school with kids of all races like the show on cable called Degrassi High." Unfortunately this was not going to be wrapped up tonight in this apartment in 42 mins with commercials this was real.

"Tyler sweetie get up, you know mommy has to go in a little early to speak to the principal." "Okay mommy, I just want some juice okay?" Well she sounded cheery maybe that talk did help her. As I listened to the water run in the bathroom, hum I thought we will keep a positive attitude today and it will be okay. It always helped to confirm I found with a positive attitude to myself first. "Mommy we have a cool apartment don't we". "We sure do Ty, I kinda like that high rise look too." "Hey a muffins, cool". I could only laugh out loud with the funny expression Tyler made on her face."Have a seat Tyler enough sillyness this morning" Tyler and I always had fun being silly in the morning or just making each other laugh. "Mommy I love you." "I love you too Ty Ty." As I seeped my coffee peering over my cup at Ty, her chocolate brown skin was so pretty to me. When Ty was young she use to tell me she wished she was a light brown like me, instead of the darker color she was. I often told her God knew I like chocolate before she was born so much that she just had to come into this world my beautiful chocolate baby. "Mommy what are you smiling about so funny for?" "Ty look at you my baby in the fifth grade, almost as tall as me." "Yeah I guess Wheaties do work huh?" "Okay miss lady, lets hurry up now, I'm already going in a little late." "Okay mommy my book bag is by the door with my coat."

Walking down the hall to the elevator I wondered how the conversation was going to go this morning at the school. As the elevators doors opened there was a young white couple in the elevator whom spoke. "Good morning." "Good morning". Riding down to the lobby I also thought of how although my supervisor was left a voicemail explaining I would be in later, so as to go to my daughter's school. How was this going to affect his opinion of this new employee already on the job two months and needing to arrive late.

Once we reached the lobby you could tell it was a workday mothers out front waiting for buses. Business men and women going to their cars in the parking lot. "Ty let me roll your book bag to the car give you a break this morning." "Mommy I got it" As we both reached for the front doors, one of the elderly ladies sitting outside reading the paper opened the door. "Good morning neighbor, hi I'm Hattie I live down the hall from you, Hi honey" "Hello I'm Janette and this is Tyler. Sorry I haven't introduced myself to you before." "Well thank you Ms. Hattie nice meeting you, you have a great day." "Yes Ms. Hattie you have a nice day." "Well thank you young lady." Approaching the car I thought how terrible it on one hand someone can show kindness so easily, and on the other people can also so easily be cruel. I wanted so much to believe this was not happening to me. "Mommy do you want me to put the book bag in the back seat or what?" "Front is fine Ty, remember you are going directly to the office with me okay?" "You won't need to drop me off at the early childcare today?" "Actually Tyler I want you there so as to speak as well. Trust me it will be okay."

Walking to the front door of the school I could see since it was early, teachers were still arriving. As I approached the front door I could see there was a buzzer directly on the building, for security reasons so I pushed the buzzer once. Since there was also a camera there apparently they had noticed me and suddenly I heard the click in the door. Immediately upon entering the office I could feel as well as sense that "what do you want look" this did not have the same vibe from the orientation that was for sure. "Good morning I would like to speak to the principal please?" A young woman looked up from her desk to ask "what is this concerning?" "Well I would prefer to speak with the principal since I have left several messages, and to no avail not contacted my her or her assistant. My name is Ms. Rusher and this is my daughter Tyler Rusher. I have left messages for my daughter's home room teacher as well." "Do you have an appointment?" "No but I do not have a problem waiting to speak to her if that would be okay". By the firmness in my voice I tried although being professional to let it be known that I was going to wait, however long. There were two other ladies in the office whom before this exchange had only looked up once. Suddenly an older woman spoke up to say, "I'm sure it would be okay." "Thank you," Tyler and I sat down. Might as well sit, because I didn't feel I was going to be asked.

It was not long before the principal arrived. As if out of earshot she walked in, very professional looking. "Good Morning, How can I help you?" Her smile was warm and sincere as she gestured for Tyler and myself to enter her office. She immediately closed the door quietly. "Good Morning and thank you for seeing me with such short notice, but this will not take long. My name is Janette Rusher and this is my daughter Tyler. She has had some problems since coming to your school. I have sent messages by Tyler. Along with calling the school, and have not been contacted. I do understand school has not been in session long but a simple respond of acknowledgement from her teacher that she at least received the notes of my concern would have been appreciated. "Well first of all lets slow down, Tyler how are you, and Ms. Rusher may I ask Tyler what has happened since she has come to our school to make her so unhappy." I realized at that moment I supposed I had spoke quite fast and could feel the adrenaline in my throat. "Yes that would be fine." At this point Tyler preceded to tell the principal about what had happened most recently in the lunchroom. Her head dropped down slowly as her eyes no longer met the principal's while speaking. "Tyler look up so she can hear you." I could see tears coming from her eyes as I observed closer. I continued to tell the principal my concerns and the fact that since the incidents I had not been contacted by the homeroom teacher as of yet. "I can assure you Ms. Rusher we want Tyler to feel welcome here and I was not aware of these situations. Tyler are you sure the girl in the lunchroom said exactly what you just said here?" At this point I felt I had to interrupt, "Why are you questioning what exactly was said to her" "Well sometimes Ms. Rusher children can take something they hear and get an entirely different interpretation from how it was intended." "Personally I don't feel that was the case here, because I know my daughter and I would hope you will nip this in the bud before it becomes an issue further." I could tell by the look on the principal's face that she was not at all happy with my response to her summation of this. Not to mention the fact that my arms were folded across my chest in a defensive matter."Ms. Rusher, how about Tyler and I find out who this young lady is that has made her so uncomfortable, and address the problem directly." Being most aware of my body language I decided to unfold my arms and sit back not so forward to be more receptive. Almost at the same time Tyler placed her hand in my lap, were our hands touched. "That sounds fine but I would however like to make an appointment with her homeroom teacher to speak to her regarding the problems she is having in her classroom as well, my concern is for my daughter to feel comfortable also and I would appreciate your help." "I will arrange for her homeroom teacher to call you and set up a time for you and her to sit down perhaps before school very soon to address your concerns" "Thank you, here are my work and home numbers where I can be contacted." "Have a nice day Ms. Rusher." "You as well and thank you again." Walking out thru the office, the ladies meekly give me half smiles as if "we sure are glad you're leaving" I purposely announced "You ladies have a nice day!" The surprise on their faces told me all I needed to know "aren't you the cute one." I am sure they had strained to listen and probably did not care for me to interrupt the routine that day. Tyler walked with me to the car in the parking lot. It really hit me the sea of white faces of children with their parents coming to be dropped off. Don't get me wrong there were some black faces but not many and according to Tyler she was the only one in her classroom. I could see how this could be overwhelming, but I was willing to hang in there. "Well Tyler I have to get to work now so I can see the kids are lining up, I love you and it will be okay." "Mommy I am sorry you are late for work." "Oh Tyler chill, you are so silly I just wanted to get to the bottom of this mess, and I feel that your principal will assist in any way she can. Remember you have to be strong. Now go get in line. Let's be positive miss lady! My fifth grader is going to be fine." "I feel better mommy thank you!" We kissed, and I watched as she hurried back to line up all the while observing the children and parents. I knew she was going to turn around anytime now to wave, and see if I was smiling back too.

Riding to work I thought of this whole dilemma I was going thru, why me why my daughter I just wanted an uneventful new year of school. Just starting a new job the last thing I needed was a distraction of this kind. I wondered how was the principal going to fix this, were the "ladies" in the office already labeling me a problem, most importantly was Tyler going to be singled out at school. The last thing I wanted or needed was for Tyler to put in a bad position at school. Pulling into the parking lot at work was uneventful just trying to get my mind together for my day at work. As I exited my car I wondered as I notice the different races of people both black, white and various nationalities enter the building, how many as children had to deal with such stupid crap. I mean here we are about to go to war with Iraq, where another country just sees us as the enemy Americans neither black nor white. Just want to kill us, but in this country we still have some stupid petty small minded people in different pockets in this country, who want to hang on to prejudice. Unfortunately my daughter was meeting some of their children.

Even though I was only on the second floor I didn't want to lug up the stairs my brief and hated stairs anyway. "Good Morning

Janette!" "Good Morning, Diane how are you this morning!"
"Ask me after several cups of coffee." As the elevator opened
we both stepped off. "Have a nice day Janette." "You too."
Diane was a very nice young white girl who actually helped me
move to my new apartment, she was so sweet we had worked
together at my previous job. Like Karry a lot of us had came
to this company since we all were being laided off. Actually
Diane was old enough to be my daughter herself, she was about
23yrs old. Just the nicest girl all I can say is very sweet. It was
so funny when she found out I was moving to the west side of
Cleveland, and volunteered to help. I asked her several times
are you sure? I will manage okay I replied she said no problem
and even offered to use her truck. Well it turned out I needed
after all the day of my move my truck was given to someone
else. So it worked out okay anyway.

There were several things I needed to do before signing on to
my phone, read emails check for any specials going on. I was
not really a coffee drinker it was just fine with me to start work
right away and take a break later. Let's see nothing new in
emails. Of course to suggestive sell additional products when
needed. The challenge of this job was learning about electronic
parts and what they do. My cubicle was a great working space,
because I had high walls, in my cube this allowed me to have
plenty charts and helpful aids. What I loved about the job
was the challenge to sell successfully to either manufacturing,
hospitals, private industry etc. This was I thought, going to be
a happy time for us, Tyler and I. I wanted to be such a good
productive mother for Tyler. We were part of our own team.

"Hey lady I sent you a email earlier, I know we have been busy
but hey can't a girl get an answer"! "Sorry Karry it's just I came
in a little later and wanted to get right on the phones." "Yeah
we have been busy nonstop." "So I guess you won't be taking
a lunch then." "No not really I wanted to work thru lunch to

make up the time I was late". "You had an appointment or something?" "Just I decided to go to Tyler's school to address some issues, with her principal. Karry I can't totally be happy at work and concentrate completely on my job if my child is unhappy." "Janette I understand that but, don't forget I mean all kids new to a school have their ups and downs I am sure it will be worked out." "Karry you make it seem all trivial and unimportant." "No I am not saying that, just you don't want to be conceived as an angry parent, I grew up in Parma and this is a great school system. Hey my grown son went to this system. Give it a chance." "Karry I really don't feel you truly understand my point here or the seriousness of this." I too believe Tyler can get a good education here. It just should be plain to you of that also. My daughter should be focused on school and right now that seems to be difficult for her." "Look my break is up, have a nice day, I'm late." The abruptness in Karry's complete turn and departure, left me knowing she was upset with my opinion. Which right now, I did not care, considering by the noise in the office the phones were quite busy. I decided to go on to my next call, and continue to work till five. Karry would see me later I was sure of.

Four-thirty came fast as I wrapped up the last call. Selling seemed to agree with me today. I found myself on auto pilot along with hoping with each call, it was Tyler's school. Maybe an appointment with her teacher, or follow up call from the principal. Might as well stretch my feet having sat all day, a quick twenty minutes I could go by Karry's cube. As I approached her cubicle Karry was half out of her cube talking to a co-worker across from her. "Hello ladies, shouldn't we be working?" "Hi Janette, I was just saying this day went fast with the call volume so steady." "Just wanted to say goodnight, took a quick break." I felt a pause in the air. Karry suddenly spoke. "This paperwork is going to take a minute. Goodnight see you in the morning." I could tell by her tone she was still a little upset about my words.

Focused on having a good evening, I would finish up my last five minutes with some follow up faxes and calls. My evening was not going to be spoiled by a tiff with a friend. I had enough to think about with Tyler tonight.

Driving home I had hoped that Tyler had a good day. Leaving the building late today 10 minutes to be exact. The last thing I wanted was to be late for pickup. Why is it just because the first few weeks my timing was great. Now for the life of me I could not get off on time at 5:00 oclock for nothing. Was traffic purposely trying to get to me as well? Although when talking to someone, I never wanted to rush a person off the phone in the middle of a sale. This was my job, I wanted to do well. Nevertheless I was going to need to get a after school pickup by someone maybe a carpool with another mom. With winter to think of, I needed to be sure I would get to her. In anticipation of this I had left a note on the mail room wall for a few days. I was cutting it quite close in picking Tyler up to 6:00pm the deadline and did not want her to have to walk.

"I'm so sorry I'm late, traffic and everything." It was all I could do to just sign Tyler out at 6:05pm. The attendant left there was already with her coat on. "Thank you so much I apologize for the lateness." "Ms. Rusher you have a nice day." I could tell by her tone she just wanted to go home. In other words just get your child miss. No until today did my shoes hitting the hard wood floors on the gym sound so loud as I walked to the door to leave. The echo was loud as if announcing to the entire school. Not to mention it seemed extra loud today along with Tyler's rolling bookbag across the floor. I didn't know it squeaked until today. "Mommy why are you late today?" "Tyler I'm sorry I just got busy at work and then traffic, and well lets go honey get in the car okay." "Okay mommy, I love you." "I love you too, Ty Ty." Her smile did me good considering I had on my mind her school my lateness and wanted to asked her more about her day. That would wait until dinner.

"Mommy let me press the elevator button, please please." Tyler rushed to the elevator doors, although you could plainly see that the up button was pressed, she still pressed it anyway. Of course there was a young woman standing there waiting to go up. "Ty hold up can't you see the lady has pressed the button." "I know mommy I just like to do it anyway." The young woman smiled so politely as if amused by our exchange. With that the elevator opened. I liked our apartment on the sixth floor. We were located at the very end of the hall and today the hall seemed a lot longer. When you entered our little apartment it had a foyer and it was so cute. The living room was so large, enough for a sofa and loveseat and table with a computer along with the entertainment center. Beautiful plants adored the window that overlooked the courtyard in the back of the building. My kitchen was lovely as well actually it stretched out to a large dining room which had 2 refrigerators. One came with the apartment and the other I could not find a buyer for so I took it with me when I moved. It turned out to be quite nice because I decided that I would stock that up for winter with juices and after school snacks for Tyler. The rest of the apartment rooms were also large including the bathroom. I simply loved our apartment, Tyler did as well it was home.

"Mommy do you want me to start my home work now?" "Yeah why not Ty..I can start dinner." As Ty walked to her room I wondered because she seemed a bit chipper was school okay today. Or was she trying to hide something. Sometimes she pretended things were okay just to make me happy. Or how she put it "I know you have so much on your mind, I don't want to worry you". That was not good either because she was only 10 years old and did not need to store things up inside so young. As we set down to dinner, I looked over at Tyler she did not even look up at me as she ate. Considering it was the two of us in the apartment we always talked to each other, unless she was angry at me or me with her. That was not the case tonight. "Ty you finished your homework?" "Yes mommy, do you want me to go and get it?" "No Ty that will not be necessary. You eat I can go get it later." Suddenly Tyler stood up and went to her room down the hall, almost knocking over her chair from the table in such a huff. "Ty hey come back here eat please madam." From the dining room table I can't really say what I could hear. It was muffled but I could hear that much. Before I could turn around Tyler had returned to the table and sat down again. "Tyler what's going on here you sit down no word. Then when I ask about your homework you rush to your room and act strangely." "Mommy its messy in my room and I thought I would go and get it, that's all." "Okay Ty I guess. Tell me about school today how was it? Did the principal talk to the student that bothered you in the lunchroom?" Finally Tyler decided to look up at me with my question. "Yes mommy when I went to the lunchroom today, the principal asked me to show her the girl that said that to me. I did and then she told me to sit down and she would handle it." "What happened next?" "The principal had the girl come up to me and apologize for making me feel uncomfortable and said she was sorry." "That was very nice of the girl to do that. Did your homeroom teacher say anything to you about contacting me?" "No mommy" "Hmm.. how was the rest of your day?" "It was okay I guess, I just want to go to school mommy I want friends no one wants to be my friend. Heather is nice to me I like her. She does not make a big deal about me being black she likes me for me. Maybe if I was lighter skinned they would like me more!" "Tyler don't say that!....doesn't mommy have friends of all races? Tyler I am so sorry this is happening to you...but remember everyone in this city is not a racist. We have unfortunately come up against a few knuckle heads who are. Tyler you are a beautiful black child, be proud of your dark skin. Didn't you say you had a friend name Heather did you see her today?" "Yes, but I don't understand how someone like Heather who is white can like me with no problem mommy. Then another kid will not want to hold my hand in gym." "I was not aware of that Ty...I'm so sorry!" What to say, I didn't know what..I thought this is not happening to us. I didn't know what to say or think..did I ask for much or want much NO just my daughter to go to school in peace. Sure I expected the simple that is my ink pen, or I want to play first. Not this stupid dumb bigoted junk. I mean what else was it. Of course it exists out in the world I wasn't naïve but my child,I could see in front of my face was losing her joy of school. She questioned her color, her worth, I was trying to deal with all this. Being that she didn't mention any notes from school yet. I decided to let it go for now and just think. "Ty was there any homework today?" "No mommy." Her head was down as she searched the floor."Hey tell you what how about I make a nice taco dinner and you go lay down and listen to your cd. We will get thru this Ty, Give me a hug. Sometimes people are stupid and just don't like people they don't understand or like for whatever reason. Continue to be kind, look up at me. I love you very much and trust me it will be okay. Your open house should be coming up soon, if your teacher does not contact me before then. I promise you I will address it with her there." Ty loosed her hug of warmth and went down the hall to her room. As she disappeared in to her room, there was not that turn for her to look at me with assurance. I knew she was beginning to doubt, one of us I just didn't know whom.

Dinner was silent, but that was okay. I could tell Ty had a lot on her mind. She didn't need small talk now we both listen to the kitchen radio with its soft jazz, and the silence was fine for now. Fixing her braided hair while she sat and read a book after dinner was nice too. I just wanted her to feel the love in the room. "Mommy, can I sleep in the room with you tonight?" "Sure Ty, no problem we will pretend we are camping tonight how's that." "Okay." "So you go brush your teeth and get ready for bed and I"ll fix the bedroom." That night although I was right next to her, she was only comforted for a little while, between her content movement I could see her rest was not that ..rest. Occasionally I got up to go look out the window, looking out into the night I saw my move, my job her pain and my own loneliness, because I knew my family was not there only my own strong faith and prayer.

Morning came soon today, I felt as if I had just laid down. Ty had finally settled during the wee morning hours, but I was still tired. I leaned toward the sink in the bathroom bumping my head toward the mirror. I closed my eyes wishing I could go back to the time this summer when Tyler could not wait to swim in the pool. Sure there were more whites then blacks there too. Actually most times we were the only ones, but I showed Tyler we would ignore the stares and just have fun. I met a couple of ladies who were polite. They spoke and smiled politely, but I knew some did not want us there. Since we came so often, they too learned how to ignore us as well and Tyler and I played together. Sometimes she tried to play with other kids, but the looks and stares were bothersome to them as well. I always had time for Tyler and stood in the 4 feet end with her. You would have thought the fact that I was not all that secure in a bathing suit would have bothered me. It didn't I was determine to show Tyler it's their problem if people are going to stare. We were going to have fun.

"Mommy why are you staring in the mirror? You forgot to wake me up. What time is it?" "Tyler I'm just thinking about my day. Want breakfast madam?" "Yeah mom, want me to make your bed?" "No Ty I will be out shortly. You get your clothes laid out. I'm almost done. How do you feel today, how did you sleep?" "Not good mommy, I wish we didn"t move here from Cleveland, these kids most of them don't like me. I have just two friends, I know you said give it a chance and kids will be kids but they don't want us here. My teacher ignores my hand when I raise it, the other kids don't want to play with me. Why can't we just move again?" "Tyler hang in there, I know it's hard to understand why kids act like they do. You have to understand that kids that say prejudice things that they heard somewhere. Or were taught it. The kids that you meet that are nice to you probably in their homes they are taught to treat people with kindness and understanding. I believe that kids are not born with hate, don't you Ty?" "I guess so mommy." I mean really Ty remember when you use to go to the clinic with me when you were little around 2 or so?" "I guess so, why?" "There were kids black, white of all races you would just go up to a child and play while waiting for the doctor. You didn't care or the child what race they were, nor the parents. You would just play. Unfortunately sometimes for whatever reason kids change due to what they either hear or have been taught." "So mommy you want me to try to understand and ignore the stupid things some kids do and try harder?" "I know Ty its sounds like a lot right now but let's give it a chance." "Besides won't you miss Heather?" "Yeah mommy I would." Tyler smiled finally as I reached to hug her and kiss her forehead. "So lets get ready miss lady!" "Okay mommy."

Walking down the hall toward the elevators that morning, I focused on Tyler as she rushed to press the down button. "Hurry up mommy it's here!" "Okay Ty. I'm coming." "Look mommy, empty no stops today straight to the bottom." As I stepped in, I thought did what I spoke to Ty earlier seek in, or was she pacifying me. Sometimes she would put on a understanding front, feeling she had to. When behind that "sure mom" act she was scared inside. I had hoped I made her feel good this morning. The last thing she needed was not to feel this was going to work out. I always tried to show her sometimes true strength came from trying to endure even when it seemed difficult at times. I tried to imagine her heart and how it felt sitting in a class, where no one looks like you, but you want to fit in. Kill them with kindness I always told her. Please god let it work now.

"Ty I forgot to check the mail last night when I came in, hold up." Looking up on bulletin board, after getting my mail I noticed I had a response to my before school childcare situation. Great a phone number I would check it at lunch. "Mommy what's that?" "Well I know if I keep being late picking you up from the after school care, I am going to need an alternative for you Ty." "Hey mommy look who is outside at the front, Ms. Hattie." "Good morning, Ms. Hattie!" "Good Morning ladies!" This woman who I only new as my neighbor down the hall, seemed so nice a grandmotherly type. Tyler smiled back at Ms. Hattie with approval. When we walked to the car I turned to wave goodbye. This was a great kickoff to my monolog to Ty about people, I was glad she could see although Ms. Hattie was white, she was human first and seemed to be a nice woman. Every morning I got the impression she sat sometimes to get the paper at the front door. We didn't catch her every morning, but today it was especially welcome.

It was a happy ride to work Ty and I sang to songs on the radio and before we both knew it we were at the school. I dropped her off and she hurried to put her book bag away and play. I was determined not to let this situation get me down. Driving to work I thought this is so stupid and I will get thru this. "Good Morning Janette" "Good Morning Karry" Isn't ironic the first person I see this morning is the person who steadily sold me on the fact this is a great "apartment" it would be okay. "How's Tyler, this morning? "Actually considering everything she is staying positive and realizing that some children like people can be ignorant. The bottom line she just wants to have friends and be happy." Why did I feel the Karry thought I was referring to her as being ignorant. "Well Janette you and Tyler have a special bond and I'm sure she knows that you just want the best for her." Thru her clinched teeth smile I could tell this was a, "I will tell you what you want to hear speech." If this was another time I would have believed her statement but today, I questioned her motive. As I headed in to my cubicle I decided I would not let anything get me down today. Maybe today I would get a call from her teacher arranging a meeting for a conference, I just wanted so much for this to be behind us both and move on. After all I loved my job it was quite challenging, sell electronic parts was quite fascinating to me. The enjoyment of selling was actually fun. I felt so enpowered in my cubicle with all my graphs and charts, not to mention my desk full of plants and of course pictures of Tyler to keep my motivated.

I enjoyed so much my job, here we were all trying to sell electronic parts and it was fun, exciting at times. Especially when talking to customers, "how many resistors would you like for example". Not knowing what a resistor even looked like, of course that is where my charts came in I had plenty of visual aids and notes to compare and review. Everyone was nice and friendly and eager to help you, if you were not sure of any part you were selling. A call center is a job you either like or you don't. In my case I liked very much, the fun for me was talking to many different people and showing I was knowledgeable about the product I was selling electronic parts alongside some sales reps in the company that had actually degrees in electronics and being just as confident meant a lot to me. I was doing quite well the last thing needed on my new job was the constant distraction of Tyler being mistreated at school. I began to feel that I had no right to be happy at times when I got a nice sale, because always in the back of my mind I felt that Tyler was sitting somewhere unhappy, or god knows what she was dealing with. "Hey girl what's up with you, sent an email earlier, we going to lunch or what. You working so hard over here and all." Surprise surprise, Karrie decides to show up fake smile and all. Why did I feel that our friendship was slipping away, because I had mentioned my unhappiness with Tyler's school. "Hey I saw them I just wanted to catch up on my paperwork in between calls, sure what time would you like lunch?" "12:30 is fine with me considering we have a half hour want to go thru the drive at McDonalds and talk on the way?" I knew this was her way of trying to apologize for now being sympathetic to my concerns over Tyler. I remember at our old job, there was always a smile and words of encouragement coming from one of us to each other, in whatever problem the other was having. I remember Karry suffering a personal loss of a family member passing and she looked so drained as she walked thru out the office. I made a special effort to stop and talk to her and give my condolences to her. Karry always came across to me as a compassionate person. So that's why it was so odd to see this person before me so flip at times about my daughter's dilemma. "That's sounds okay to me Karry, meet you down stairs at 12:30." "Great Janette, my breaks is just about over see you later." She abruptly trotted off with not even a question of Ty's well being. My mind continued to float back to Tyler, I was worried that her day was not going so well, I realized I had no right to expect Karry to feel the same way about Tyler as I did. For all she could see was that her childhood was great in Parma, and so what's the problem? The morning went pretty fast maybe because I had so much on my mind or just busy. Calls were coming fast and furious it was all I could do to immediately address the accounts on the line and pull up the correct electronic part to sell. Whew lunchtime finally. I was never so glad to pull off that headset. I was ready for lunch today.

"Your car, or mind, Janette." "How about yours Karry you have the air conditioner." "Sure Janette." All the while she drove and spoke I never heard a thing my mind drifted back to Tyler.

No calls from the teacher on my voice mail or cell phone. It bothered me no calls were coming in from the teacher to meet or address my concerns. "Janette are you listening to me or what? You seem far away!" "Of course Karry I hear you." "Oh really what did I just say then?" "Okay I give up I'm sorry, I have Tyler on my mind." "I know it Janette, but trust me it will be okay. Just give it time." "We'll see Karry, I sure hope so Tyler means so much to me." "I know Janette, I am a mother too remember." Riding back to work I just tried to smile and listen to Karry, rattle away talking about her plants and different gardening passions going on at home. So just nodding and smiling was fine with her. She basically wanted someone just to be listening. Which was fine with me for my thoughts were elsewhere.

I was very disappointed to see that no voicemail lights showed up on my phone once I returned. Maybe as the saying goes no news is good news, yeah right. Staring down at Tyler's picture on my desk I decided to concentrate on the positive, just work diligently this afternoon and look forward to seeing my daughter later. The afternoon flew by already 4:45. Let's see a break from the calls, might as well check email. Hm, nice to see Karry still has a sense of humor. "Dear Janette you were so talkative at lunch could not get a work in edge wise. Thanks for lunch, Karry p.s. believe me things will get better."

Walking to my car I felt great considering it was 5:10 and I had time to get Tyler by 6:00. I really didn't need to arrive late. "Mommy." Tyler just lifted me up when she called out my name so excitedly. If I was having a bad day any day. Hearing her and seeing her smile meant the world to me. "Okay Ty Ty calm down." Athough Tyler was tall for her age. I was always like any mom , I saw her as my baby plus it reassured me that maybe with the smile on her face she might have had a great day. "Hi baby, how was your day?' I watched as her head lowered to the floor speaking to the floor boards beneath her. "It was okay I guess mommy. Let's just go okay." Her tones lowered as she spoke. As Tyler raised her head up, I could see the tears well up in her eyes. "What is it Ty?" "Mommy let's just go okay please." Ty pulled on me bragging to go now. She gripped my hand tightly. "Okay Ty get your things while I sign you out." All I could think of was what now. It was hard for me not to look around the gym and not search the faces of the adults to see any clues. They seem oblivious to my look of concern. "Ready Tyler I'll get your bookbag." "Okay mommy." Tyler hurried to the exit as I said goodnight to the ladies, and followed her swiftly so as not to be left behind. Outside I immediately hugged her tight letting her cry out her pain. Standing there I felt that I was failing Tyler she didn't ask for this, all she wanted was to go to school and have friends just like any other 10 yr old. I looked down at her braids so neatly parted and stroked her head. "Mommy I didn't want to cry in front of the other kids. I wanted to be brave for you." "Tyler it's okay let's just go home we'll talk later okay." I slowly opened the car door trying not to let Tyler see my hurt on my face, as she go into the car. Tyler had enough on her mind she didn't need the added guilt of feeling this was all her fault. As I drove home from the school Tyler sat in the back just looking out the window. I tried not to look at her thru the rear view mirror too much, so as not to make it so obvious I was so upset. Why my child! She dressed cute like the other kids. Was friendly nice, just wanted friends I felt I was completely helpless. Me always trying to lead by example. Yeah right so what I have friends of all races what good that did Tyler now. She could not understand this whole racism thing. Coming into the parking lot, I wondered who would speak first. I didn't want to rush the conversation. I decided to try and park closer to the building this evening making it easlier for Ty. She seems not only unhappy, but tired too. I knew that already this was not going to be a welcome conversation this evening, Tyler was neither talkative or asked about the radio station. Her thing always when she got into the car was to change the station while talking a mile a minute. I immediately unlocked the doors after parking and rushed to assist Tyler with a smile, out of the passenger door.

"Hey young lady want to skip to the front door?" "No mommy kind of tired tonight." Real bright Janette can't you see she's tired. "I'm sorry Tyler, you do look drained Ty, come here baby I love you so much." I pulled Tyler closer to me as we walked to the front door. "Mommy you don't have to pull my book bag too." "Oh Tyler I like how the wheels light. So chill out kiddo." "You are so silly mommy!" "Oh no do I see a smile?" As we both walked thru the doors. It was nice to see Tyler light up a bit. "Mommy shouldn't we check the mail?" "Sure Tyler why not." "Look mommy there is a note on the bulletin board about after school care, didn't you say you wanted to find someone?" "Hm let's see Ty, Oh look Ty there is a lady on our floor who is looking for children before and after school for childcare." "You going to call her mommy." "Maybe Ty, lets first get up stairs okay, I'm sure you are tired and hungry so am I. "Mommy I got the elevator button!" It was nice to see Ty's mood lighten up somewhat as we entered the elevator. Ty leaned into me it was so apparent how much she depended on me for courage and to stand by her. However this situation was going to turn out I was not under no circumstances going to let Tyler down. "Come on mommy 6th floor we'll here." Strolling down the hall to our apartment, I thought maybe Tyler would bring up whatever disturbed her earlier at school, or should I bring it up first. "Mommy let me use my key." "Okay madam." "Put your book bag in your room Ty, and start your homework okay." "Sure mommy." I watched Tyler walked to her room pulling her book bag, behind her I knew in my heart she was trying to put on a brave front. I decided to check my emails, right away; I had given my email address to Ty's teacher along with the cellular number. Hm no email. That's just great I thought!

"Mommy here's a note from school; I think it's about an open house coming up, mommy you can talk to the teacher then right...about the stuff in school right?" As I read the note, I thought this was going to be my opportunity to speak to her teacher directly. There was indeed an open house coming up and I was definitely going to be there! It made sense, I mean school was only in for about couple of months and it was time for open house.

"Ty come to dinner, you finish with your home work yet?" "Yes mommy." Why is it as I tried to go into Ty's room while asking her if she was ready for dinner. Was she quickly closing her desk draw so as to not let me see what she was doing. "Ty what's that you have there?" Pointing to the black magic markers on her hands. "Nothing mommy I will just go and wash my hands now." Tyler rushed passed me hurriedly to the bathroom. I didn't know what was up, maybe a class project, or knowing her she was probably making me some kind of poster or card for me. Oh well I wouldn't want to spoil the surprise. "Tyler how was school today? That note you gave me was for open house coming up tomorrow night." Tyler stared a moment at her orange juice on the table. I didn't want to rush the response either. I continued to eat dinner as if knowing any moment she would speak. "Mommy today I was in gym and we had to pick teams, and no one picked me to be on a team. It really hurt I wanted to cry. I hate that school I don't want to go back there. Why do we have to stay here? No body wants us here." The whole time Tyler spoke she never looked up from the orange juice, it was if she in a trace. The whole answer was monotone, as if she knew it didn't matter what she said, I could tell. She didn't want to hear my answer. All the wind was out of her sails. I could tell. "Tyler what happen in gym was awful, did the gym teacher do anything to fix the problem?" "Mommy the gym teacher is really nice, she made one of the teams take me." "Tyler what do you mean take?" "She just told the kids

35

that what they were doing was selfish and then she rearranged the teams." Tyler started to cry. I felt like whatever I said would probably sound bland to Tyler at this point. "Tyler I'm glad the gym teacher made it fair, however that does not excuse what the kids did. Do you have any friends at all at school Ty?" "Yeah my friend Heather she is very nice. She has spiked hair and is always trying to be my friend; she told some of the kids they were stupid for not liking me." "Tyler wipe your tears I know all of this is hard. I promise you somehow we will get thru this. When I go to the open house I'll make a point of seeing the gym teacher and tell her thank you. Along with speaking to your homeroom teacher, about these consistent problems." I reached across the table to grab Tyler's hands. Her head hung down the entire time she was speaking. "Look at me Ty trust me please. I know you have heard this all before, but mommy will fix this." Her head lifted up with my words. "Don't feel that each time you tell what is going on at that school, I blame you or think it is your fault. Like I told you before some people are just ignorant. Even so Tyler you must remember a lot of this anger some of these kids have, come from what they have heard maybe stereotypes of what all black people are about. Or perhaps just that old saying if you don't understand something you push it away or dislike it. Some kids may think it's so cool to hate black people, for example since my friend dislikes her so should I. When I go to the open house tomorrow night I will try and address this Tyler okay?" Tyler seemed to focus directly at me, as if she was telling me telepathically mommy I do trust you. I loved my daughter so much as I just wanted so much not to fail her. "Let's enjoy our dinner Ty, be positive I refuse to believe every white child in your school is prejudice. Because if that were the case, then you would have to believe that in an all black school, all black children are prejudice, and you and I know what is not true. Don't you agree?" "Well yeah mommy, I see what you mean a few kids and their parents with negative attitudes, make it bad for a whole group." "Believe me Tyler when I say I can't guarantee a change in the way people or kids will treat you in the future, but we will not let this defeat us. Continue to be kind regardless of the kids that are mean, and if it gets too hard to bare you keep raising your hand to tell the teacher, I don't care how annoyed she gets. You always show respect, but yes due report all negative actions okay." "Right mommy! After dinner Ty, and I went over her homework and played a little with her dolls. I loved to make Tyler laugh by pretending her dolls talked to me by holding their heads to my ear. She would look at me as if I had no sense. Then I would nod my head in agreement, as if they were telling me something.

While tucking in her that night, I was curious as to what was in the drawer Ty so hurriedly closed up in her drawer. Do I trust Tyler and assume it's nothing , or go and be nosey by peeking in her dresser drawer. I just had to know. Wouldn't you know as I reached for the drawer Ty moved and shifted in her bed. I quietly tipped out of the room. I would have to come back later.

Looking around my apartment I had the feeling of being so alone. Although Tyler was in the next room. I was so alone in my heart, in the sense that there was no one in my family that I felt supported me. I could hear my mother and father now. "No one told you to move over there anyway." My sister whom I already had a strained relationship with , I sure she didn't want to talk. We weren't even close or my brothers whom were in their own worlds doing their own thing. I could deal with the loneliness but I guess it was most hard on Tyler. Having no uncle or an aunt to confide in or even call. My family was dysfunctional, much like a lot of other families regardless of the race. Of course in person we never showed it. Oh in public everyone appeared so happy and all smiles. It really hurt that I had no one to talk to for support. Had I made a stupid decision to move over here, without thinking it entirely thru? But I loved my job and just wanted to be near my home. After all we live in a world of all races, we work in that world. I was not knocking people of any race wanting to go to a predominately all black or white school. That's fine if you prefer that. There are people like myself who chose to live where they want and exposing their children to different cultures. Why should my child be made to feel like an outcast just because she is black in a predominately white school. I mean I was not naïve to the fact that prejudice will never be totally erased in this society. Whether it's black against white, or white against black. As I stared out from my bedroom window into the dark night watching the cars go by, I thought about the fact that too many people forget or either don't care that this country works because of its diversity. Here we defend the United States against any and all negative combatants standing shoulder to shoulder, but on the other hand just me and my daughter moving to this suburb really upset some people. It's so unfortunate in this country that there are still pockets of racism lurking around the corner to remind us, that we still have a lot of work to be done to educate people, not to get too comfortable. I was beginning to feel cheated of the joy of my new apartment. The excitement of Tyler learning new things, and meeting new people. One good thing I was so glad that had come out of the move was her learning the saxophone, her new friend Heather who just liked her for her. Oh yeah Tyler said Heather had blond spiked hair and she was oh so cool.

While staring out the window, I realized I still had the note to call this woman back that was interested in baby sitting Tyler, a Mrs. Zarina, I wondered if that was her first name. Let's see only 9:45 maybe it's not too late to call. As I dialed the number it didn't occur to me what this person's ethnicity was until she swiftly answered. "Hello" "Hello my I speak with Mrs. Zarina?" "Speaking, whom am I speaking to?" "Hi my name is Janette Rusher and I live here in the building and understand that you are looking for children before and after school for childcare. Do you live in this building were your note was posted?" "Yes actually on the 6th floor." "So do I." As we talked she told me more about her, her apartment number and the fact she was married and her husband was a math teacher in Cleveland. She was a homemaker, her and her husband had moved here from India over a year ago. There was recruiting done apparently for strong teachers with a math background and her family wanted to come to Cleveland already having family here. The more we talked I found out she had a son in the 5th grade also. She asked me if the fact that she was of Indian decent was that a problem, to which I replied of course not. I told her I was a black woman and was that a problem to which she replied no also. What was interesting as well as ironic was the fact that we immediately needed to know whether our races mattered. She also provided me with several references of the two other children she kept their parents as well as a former child's parent's number she kept for the summer that had moved away. "Sure I would love to come and meet you tomorrow, bye bye." I figured I would take Tyler with me to get her opinion of the woman, as well as see the interaction between her and Tyler. Turns out she lived on the same floor as myself and had seen Tyler and I get on the elevators before. Mrs. Zarina sounds nice I thought this is too good to be true. Finding a sitter on the same floor and her cost was great. I hoped this would work out.

"Morning Ms. Ty Ty," "Good morning mommy." "How did you sleep Ty?" "Okay mommy." "How about you?" "Well Ty I actually went to bed late I called the lady who left the note in the mailroom Ty." Tyler looked so eager for more information as she walked into the bathroom she paused. "Missy you go get ready for school." I gently shoved Ty into the bathroom, while she smiled. "I'll tell you more about the conversation at breakfast Missy." While fixing breakfast I hoped this neighbor of mine turned out to be okay. I figured I would check the references during lunch at work. "Sit missy breakfast is served." "Mm mommy." When I sat down I couldn't help but notice Tyler seemed to be in a great mood this morning. Which was good considering most mornings so far she dreaded to go to school. "Well Ms. Tyler, the lady lives right down the hall from us on the same floor." "Really." "Absolutely missy, which is even more easier for us both. Here pass me your glass for some juice." "I decided I would call her references during lunch." "What's that mommy?" "Well the lady keeps 2 other children and has given me the names of the other mothers in order for me to call and speak to me about her childcare. That way before I meet with her in person I have a little information and you can go along too to meet her and the other children."

Dropping Tyler off at the before school childcare was uneventful. I had advised Tyler I would definitely be coming to the open house this evening to address any problems as well as give her a pep talk about keeping her head and attitude up. I couldn't help but continue to notice the change in Tyler's face expression when I pulled up to the school each day. Her demeanor in general for school. My heart sank as I watched her get out the car and unlike the other kids in the school yard no other children rushed up to greet her as the exited the car. I kissed Ty and hugged her trying to reassure her it was going to be all right. Even though the school yard was quickly filling up with parents dropping their kids off, I could see Tyler just slowly walking to get in line. I also felt tears coming into my eyes, I was glad Tyler was far enough away she could not see them. Tyler turned back toward where I was parked and waved back at me. I smiled and waved back mouthing I love you to her. There was a half smile I could see on her face it was evident she didn't want to be here and I could see how she felt so ostracized just watching no interaction with other kids. Just looking at Tyler I wanted to get out of my car and so to speak "rescue" her from sea of loneliness. Instead I got out my car to wave again at Tyler as she entered the building.

Pulling into the parking lot at work, I had decided to be positive today. At lunch I would call the references from the lady in my building. Exiting my car I could see it was cloudy, but that was not going to affect me. I had to be strong for Tyler. Open house couldn't start soon enough this evening for me. It may have been cloudy outside but I was functioning on adrenaline today. Maybe it was seeing Tyler walk slowly pulling her backpack behind her to get in line, not one child approached her to say hi, or the fact that if anything some parents along with kids just looked at her strangely. Even so I wished this would all go away, but I knew it wasn't. A part of me just wanted to scream and yell, and declare how dare they hurt my daughter's heart.

Settling in at my desk I immediately signed on early. I wanted to get my emails read quickly and out of the way. I was focused I still had a job to do in spite of the turmoil around my child and me. I was her father and mother and that was all that mattered.

"Good morning, Janette." "Good morning Karry." "Sounds like you're in a good mood today." "Actually I am, I found possibly a new childcare provider for Tyler in my building, that happens to be on the same floor." "What happen to the after school care you currently have at her school?' "Well with me getting out of work late sometimes, you know with calls sometimes running over it is best to just get someone in the building. Plus the idea situation would be someone with a child at the same school, which she does happen to have!" "This lady you mean." "Of course, so I plan to call her today." "You're right sometimes that 4:45 call will take you to 5:15 especially if they are buying a lot of products." "Right, so I'm looking forward to calling her references during lunch." "Okay, I guess you won't be taking lunch then." "No not really, also I forgot to tell you there is open house tonight I'm looking forward to meeting with Ty's teacher." "She hasn't contacted you yet?" "Unfortunately not, but I am being positive so as to address it this evening. Any way I"ll talk to you later let me get started on work." "Good Luck with everything." "Thanks."

While checking my emails, I noticed that the call center lights were steadying lit up. Hmm must be sale going on. Sometimes the company sent out to the steady customers a mailing blitz to stimulate a lot of business from the latest catalog. These were usually the customers whose businesses ordered large invoices with huge supplies on a regular basis. One thing that was great about my job on the phone, was the fact there was a 5 second delay where the introduction of my name came in along with a greeting, giving me time to get ready for the call. This worked great for me. I was so pumped up; right now all I wanted to do was for Tyler as well as myself was for this new babysitter hopefully to work out. I wanted to like her along with Tyler. The calls today was for the most part were great, because I was able to do a lot of suggestive selling. This made my sales average even higher during the peak business hours of the day. I loved talking to people so I was able to build a great rapport with the customers along with motivating them about new products. The morning just flew by. I looked up and it was lunch.

I was lucky enough to reach both references Mrs. Zarina had provided for me. It turned out the ladies also lived in the building but on different floors. They raved about how kind and considerate she was. I also found out the reason that these ladies had decided to have her keep their children was how convenient her hours were before and after school. This was great considering Mrs. Zarina would transport the kids to school, along with waiting for them after school. My next concern was making sure she had insurance, along with the fact I didn't want my child in an over-crowed car. Both ladies were briefed about me calling them, so they were both forth coming and eager with info. While listening to each ladies chatter about how nice Mrs. Zarina was I wondered how they would react to me being black. My mind was made up if everything worked out. I mean I felt somewhat at ease, but of course until I actually meet with her I could not be sure. Please God let this be okay.

During the afternoon the calls slowed down, enabling me to catch up on paperwork. I looked forward to meeting with Tyler's homeroom teacher. This evening I wanted to be productive, nipping all the stupid problems in the bud. Yes I wanted to see the curriculum and chart Tyler's progress, but this meant nothing if Tyler's state of mind was not truly focused.

No, I was not going to be defensive, just a concerned parent that wanted answers. Yes I knew my child was not the only child in her classroom, but I definitely felt by now her teacher should have made an effort to contact me. Tyler had mentioned how she felt slighted in class when she raised her hand to answer a question. Along with the fact if she did answer a question wrong she was made to feel worse by the teacher, according to Tyler being told you "wasted" my time with your hand. Sure I could have said "Tyler suck it up, and deal you are not the first child to be faced with such prejudice, but no I refuse to do that.

Of course I told her to ignore the stupid gestures and comments made by kids on the playground as much as possible but enough is enough. Every parent knows their child, and when a complete turn around in attitude about school happened. I felt I needed to be more concerned and pro-active in addressing these issues.

As I answered calls thru out the afternoon, I couldn't help but think look at all I am going thru. When this move was suppose to be a simple new apartment, new school and new job. The excitement was beginning to fade. Tyler looked up so much to me. I wanted to solve all of this confusion at once, was I going to be able to?

Whew, just in time 5:55pm. At least Ty was not the last child here today. "Hi mommy?" "Hi baby." I lowered my head to sign the sheet for dismissal; I could see the woman in attendance busy fixing a child's shoe over the table. "Good evening." "Oh I'm sorry good evening, I didn't see you, how are you Mrs. Rusher?" "Oh fine thank you, how was Tyler today?" "Okay, she was playing with her friend Heather today, I guess they love Barbie." "That sounds like Tyler, you have a nice evening." "Thank you, you too!" I could see Ty pulling her book bag, toward me. "Ready mommy." "Okay Ms. Ty." While walking out to the parking lot, I hoped Ty's day had been better. "Mommy I have a note about the open house tonight, here." When Tyler entered the car I gathered the note from her hand. "Okay missy you know the routine buckle up madam." Walking around the car I hoped this was not only a reminder, but also a note saying she was eager to talk to me since I had not heard a response yet. Nope, just that a reminder about the open house time of 7:00pm. "Tyler how was your day today, any problems?" "Mommy I try to ignore the kids that don't like me." "What do you mean Ty?" "Well like when we go for bathroom break, we can get water too. So some kids won't drink from the water fountain I have used because, I hear then say mean things about my color. Like maybe it will wash off on the fountain or something stupid like that." "Tyler first let me say, you are right it's stupid, and second you are right to ignore them. I am proud of you Tyler." Tyler looked up at me and gave a half smile as we pulled into the parking lot. I responded with a smile back. As I parked the car, I felt I needed to hug her. So I reached over and embraced her. "I love you mommy," "I love you too Ty, I heard you played with Heather today, your friend. Is that right?" "Yeah, she is so cool, she says her parents taught her to like all people and it's nothing wrong with being different." "You know Ty I like her already, maybe I can meet her tonight at the open house if she comes you think?" "Mommy maybe so!" I prepared a quick snack for Ty and I to have, I reminded myself that whatever was said positive or negative I would not react unproductive. I had made the conscious decision to make sure my concerns were addressed. After all, the most important thing to remember was the fact I cared about my child's mental progress.

Pulling into the parking lot I couldn't help but notice I was not the only parent who decided to bring their child. The parking lot was filling up fast. However it was interesting how the parents, like their kids just like looked at me as if I did not belong. I could even see on their faces that question of "where's she going?" It's not like I was the only black parent there I'm sure. I just did not see any but me. This whole stupid staring at me just made me smile more and clutch Tyler's hand that much tighter. "Mommy I'll show you where my homeroom teacher is okay." "Sure Tyler, I can't wait to see her." As we both walked into the building there was a PTA table up. The ladies smiled and were very receptive and nice. While handing out the program I was told to have a nice evening. "You have a nice evening also." I responded. "That was nice of her mommy wasn't it?" "It sure was Tyler, very nice, Tyler you would have to be on the second floor wouldn't you missy?" "Mommy take your time, we'll get there soon enough." Once we reach the second floor you could see the rush of parents crowding around to the different rooms. Tyler immediately pointed out her homeroom teacher. It was interesting that as we walked toward her she purposely averted her eyes downward to the sign in table. I thought this was odd considering I raised my hand in a hello fashion with a smile. I took this to mean that maybe she was preoccupied with getting the right parents in the correct room's etc. I decided to go ahead to walk in and have a seat anyway. I looked around the room, the chairs were arranged in rows across the room. Tyler and I sat midway in the row of seats. I noticed that as people entered the room they seemed to purposely sit as far away from us as possible. Sure one can say first people were filling up the seats where they wanted to sit. I agree no problem. Of course it become obvious what was happening, when the room got quite full and the only seats were around Tyler and I. I actually found this to be quite funny. At the door I noticed a young woman with and her son walk in, they looked to be of Indian decent. I thought of the lady I was to meet later, she smiled at me. "Thank you for coming everyone, lets get started." "Tyler." I whispered. "Isn't that your homeroom teacher?" "Yes mommy, the other two teachers next to her I have for technology and science." While the introductions got under way, I looked behind the teacher's and noticed a smart board, basically it is an electronic blackboard which has a large screen with graphics to explain class activities. What I gathered from the introduction was that all three of the teacher's taught in the fifth grade, as well as the fact they all grew up in Parma. There were the stories of how proud they were of the school system. The fact unlike some other school systems in the news, they were not on strike. Along with the pronounced statement we were in the business of teaching. As Tyler's homeroom teacher spoke of the school on strike, she made a point of looking directly at me as if to say "aren't you glad you'll not there." The school system that she was referring to was predominately black. So there was no issue as to what she meant. I mean it was currently in the news absolutely daily, so you couldn't avoid knowing what she was talking about. Ty's homeroom teacher went on to introduce the other teachers and the curriculum was passed out explaining the year. It was also advised that no question and answer was going to be allowed due to time constraints. That's why the sign in sheet along with an area for conferences, either nights and days. Parents were advised to sign up on the way out. I didn't really like this open house method. I felt that the parents were made to feel like spectators and the teachers were lecturing us about the lessons they taught our kids. Whatever happened to the old school method of waiting in line with each teacher, and talking and introducing yourself briefly. Well so much for my day, before you knew it the open house was dismissed. I tried although there were many parents there to walk up to Tyler's teacher, so as to quickly address, my concern. To be only hustled away by her saying "please sign the sheet for a conference, I do not have time." I grabbed Tyler's hand and signed the sheet. It's interesting; her teacher never even looked up.

That night I just decided to concentrate on my job, and just get Tyler ready for bed. I figured for one night at least, I would act as if we were the happiest family in the world. I wanted to put aside any fears about Tyler and school right now. This could not be something negative to my child. The next morning I got Ty up right away and she was in a solemn mood. I didn't want to drudge up any bad vibes now. We both got ready in silence, listening to our own footsteps down a carpeted hall still I felt I could hear her thoughts. There was a great deal to think about today. Why did the teacher react the way she did? Was she sending me an unwritten message, or was I just being paranoid? First of all, I was not being paranoid, it did not go the way I wanted it to. I cared a great deal about my child's welfare, after all I just went to open house and feel I know even less about her classes and her how her teacher felt about her.

"Ty, want to walk to the ladies apartment down the hall with me and see what she is like with me?" I wanted to make the walk light hearted, considering I did not know her thoughts. I swing Ty's hand, waiting for a response. "Sure are you going to leave me with her today?" "No actually Tyler I want to interview her and talk to her in person and see the reaction she has to you and I." "Sort of like seeing if she is for real, and really likes kids and stuff?" "You are kind of right." "Okay" Passing the elevator I hoped that the vibe I got on the phone was right, I felt that she wanted to help me and something about it all seemed right. That was hard to say considering what was happening around.

I immediately knocked on the door, loudly but about business. If it could seem that way, from inside I could hear movement and footsteps to the door. "Hello, you are Ms. Rusher?" "Yes." "So you must be Tyler?" I watched her closely as Tyler's eyes met with hers. Ty let out a half then whole smile, I searched her eyes for any doubt or fear. There were none. "Hi". I knew that soft hi, it meant she seems nice mommy I like her. "Come in this is my son Amir." I looked to my right as I entered her apartment and saw a small young boy of Indian descent who gave me a timid but friendly hi.

"Hi Amir," I watched as Tyler walked over to the young man and extended out her hand. Amir's mother and I watched closely to see the children interact. I noticed we smiled at the same time, as the children started to talk between each other. I took a seat with Amir's mother opposite the kids. We could both see they liked each other, Tyler asked Amir something about the book he had in his hand, and I noticed they both laughed. This was good, I thought.

I paid close attention to Ms. Karina as she talked about her life, how she came to this country. I looked around the apartment and could see her beautiful decorating of the rooms. You could see her proud heritage in her apartment, it was interesting that as I looked back at her the only difference in her tone of brown and mine was she was of Indian descent and I was black. We talked for 30 mins or so and I had decided to start to leave

Tyler on the next day. She would pick Ty up after school. I would leave her at her school in the mornings. Then of course Ty would be picked up after school. I found I really felt at ease with Ms. Karina, I felt Ty would be fine.

Work was uneventful, except for the thought continuing going thru my head about Tyler's teacher. She was going to speak with me rather she liked it or not. I WAS going to make sure of that.

I kissed Ty as she went hung up her coat the ride was silent, I knew Ty was wondering if I was going to react. I parked the car very close to the front door, and found myself concentrating on what to expect. Yes I decided that I would go to the school unannounced, maybe to try and get to meet with the teacher and the principal as well. "Mommy why is it you are not going to work today?" "Aren't you going to be late?" Tyler looked up at me with surprised, searching for an answer. "Well Ty I decided that I would just try to speak with the teacher, early before class. How do you feel about that?" "Good, mommy maybe she can see you."

Walking into the principal's office, I did not like the looks I got from the other ladies who worked there. "Can I help you?" To my right the lady spoke up with a bothered look. "Yes I would like to speak with my daughter's teacher, Ms. Kent. I know that I do not have an appointment but it is pressing that I speak with her." I tried to give the appearance immediately of someone without a smile, just wanted what I wanted, I did not want to hear anything not positive. The woman looked at me, and just decided to just usher me to the seat next to the principal's office. I made sure to not look at anyone for any facial disapproval. I was determined to see Ty teacher today. Ty just sat next to me and waited. No sooner had I sat down and there was the principal approaching us both. I can only assume that someone had alerted her of my waiting for her. "How are you Mrs. Rusher, would you like to step into my office? "I stood and smiled, with Ty's tight grip. "Yes thank you, I would like to speak to Ty's teacher. I am pressed for time and want to see her teacher this morning before class. This is not making me too happy that Tyler had some issues that need to be addressed I feel right now." I rapidly, and purposely set a fast pace tone, so as to get a swift reaction from the principal. While she look at Ty with a smile, as to disarm me. I immediately decide to speak again. "I feel that Tyler's concerns are not being addressed. Basically my child is unhappy about school and I would like to speak to Ms. Kent now please."

There was a quick silence in the small office that was over just as quick. "Well Mrs. Rusher I will just call up to Tyler's teacher and find out if she is there." I watched as the principal checked her sign in roster or something like that. She then motioned for the lady whom first greeted me to escort my daughter and I to Ms. Kent. As Tyler and I climbed the stairs to the second floor, I tried to calm myself. I did not want to appear not having a open mind about anything I was about to hear, I heard the echo of my high heels hitting the steps, it was quite early and not any of the other children were in the halls. I could see as I passed the windows going up that they were in the courtyard laughing and playing and lining up. This was a fairly nice school just, that now I felt with echo of my heels with Ty's tennis shoes sneaking along side. I felt no happiness right now. It did not help that the woman stepping one step quicker in front of me did not say a word the whole time. "Mommy this is my room." I take it that the announcement from my daughter meant that the woman walking along side could now leave. For that is what she did without a word. It was apparent I was a bother to some. "Come in Mrs. Rusher, I have been expecting you." "You have?" "Well I just got a call from the principal, saying you had some concerns to address." As Ms. Kent directed my daughter and

I to come in to the classroom. Why did I feel like this was not going to go well.

I kissed Tyler as she walked to her classroom. She then gave me a quick hug, and went to her desk. Sometimes it was hard to see the look on her face, knowing that she was trying to be brave and strong for me. When I looked too long I just felt nothing but guilt, because I had placed her there. "Have a seat Mrs. Rusher, I am so sorry that I was not able to talk to you last night at the Open House. It goes so fast and that is why we like for parents to schedule conferences with us." We both sat at the same time, and then we just looked directly at each other. I knew that this short silence was to try and size it other up. "Yes that may be true." I spoke. "But right now I am just trying to get to the bottom of why she is so unhappy, she tells me about how the other children on the playground kick dirt on her, and sometimes call her the "n" word in this class." I cut my look to Tyler and back to her at once, to get her reaction. I thought that I could read her face before she spoke, to try and shed some idea about her. "I know nothing about those things that you have mentioned, what I have here are some test scores about Tyler's class work and homework." Ms. Kent had papers in front of her, and just was so focused on what she had before her. I decided that I would not like her take me off track. "Let's see these papers; I am sure that this must reflex her unhappiness with how she is being treated." After that remark I looked at Ms. Kent sternly and of course a frown of concern. "Tyler would you come over her to mommy and sit down, since this concern's you I would like for you to talk to Ms. Kent and mommy." Ms. Kent did not like the fact that I was taking some type of charge here and wanted to place Tyler next to me. I could see by the intimidating look she gave Tyler, I knew this woman was not to be trusted. "Tyler look up honey, it's okay don't look so sad." I shoot Ms. Kent a grin so as to let her know I was already aware she had a negative attitude coming from her. "Ms. Kent

I have looked at Tyler's papers and yes she is having problems with her math, but I do not see that you have tried to assist her in anyway. All I ever see is the fact that you are not returning my calls or notes that I have sent to the school for you." "Ms. Rusher I do not know what school system Tyler came from but it is apparent that she had many weak skills, in key areas that are required in the fifth grade. I feel that Tyler needs to be able to take proper criticism without disputing the outcome. Along with the fact Tyler has a body order, is it coming from her hair and clothes? I am getting complaints from children it is hard for them to focus. Maybe it is the braids in her head?" The body language that I had just observed from this woman in front of me was one of, "I am more superior than you so shut up and listen."

"I actually feel that you are missing the point here, she is being taunted in class, and that you ignore her hand. Along with the fact that she feels that you try to make her feel stupid if she does not know the answer. The bottom line is I want Tyler to have friends here, and feel that she can go to her teacher if there is a problem. Just the fact, that she gets no response from you when she says that she is called a racial slur. This bothers and concerns me deeply." Ms Kent looked directly at Tyler as if she was to response. "Tyler don't you feel that you should shoulder some of the blame as to why you are having a rough time in class?" Tyler started to tear up, this I thought was not happening right in front of me. "Excuse me Ms. Kent I feel that you should direct all your responses right now to me, and not my daughter!" "Ms. Rusher what did you expect moving into this neighborhood, I mean she is the only black child in this class!" I stood up abruptly. "Are you saying I have no right to be here?" I could see tears in Tyler's eyes she had grabbed my hand and stood up with me. Along with her tears I could see the reflection of my own, and was speechless. The bell rung at that point and I pulled Tyler outside the classroom with me. I could hear Ms. Kent saying something in the background. But over the children screaming with excitement coming up the stairs I could not hear what she was saying. Tyler clutched me so tight as the children passed up going into the room. I had to contain myself quickly. "Tyler please let me go honey it will be alright." "No mommy no, I don't want to stay here, please can I come with you? It was so hard to leave Tyler at the school that day. I remember having to pry her fingers off me, and just looking back I can still see her little fingers so tight gripping me. I had held her close and tight enough to whisper, "it will be all right Ty, I must go now, be strong baby."

As I walked to my car in the parking lot, I feel this situation was something out of a movie. Did I actually just have a teacher question my right to be here? This could not be happening; Tyler's face haunted me all day at work that day. What was I going to do? The nerve of this teacher, her whole attitude was one of not wanting to have to be bothered with my daughter. I felt that she already had it in her mind, Tyler and I had no right there. I also felt look what I had put my daughter into. She had to deal with this all day, and feel she was not wanted there. Thoughts while working, no matter what I was doing always drifted back to Tyler. What was I going to do? No matter how many times I asked myself that question, the fact remained. My daughter was not going to feel welcome for the moment. I didn't want to think that all the teachers in this school were this way. Just this women, why was she a teacher? Or was the fact she had a deep prejudice toward Tyler and me, no matter what I said or did or even Ty. She wanted to be who she was, with no regard as to how it looked or sounded of course in close quarters. I will never forget that gut feeling of being kicked right in front of your child. I was supposed to be her protector, and make things all right. Did I show weakness with my stunned looked and only tears in my eyes too? What was Tyler thinking at this time right now in school?

I knew that I was going to try and speak with the principal as soon as possible about this teacher's attitude. I was not going to stand for Ms. Kent, just speaking to me as if we did not have a voice or count. Although it was a very busy day, I still kept seeing Ms. Kent up in my face, with her smirk and smart look as if she just did something to be proud of. I made several calls to the principal and left messages for her to call me back. This whole situation seemed to be out of control. I thought that I was going in to the school to talk to the teacher to get some sense of this craziness and she is just as nutty!!!

When will this day be over? How was Tyler going to fair with the new baby sister? What kind of mess was this all turning out to be? I could not keep the picture out of my head of Tyler pulling at my clothes. The way she looked up at me for answers, and the fact I had to leave her. I know it must have looked to Tyler like I did not care. What kind of mother was I to put her in this situation? But then why was I blaming myself, I just wanted my daughter to be treated fairly. She did not have to have special treatment; I just wanted her to be treated like any other typical 10 year old in the 5th grade. This was not too much to ask. Give me a break! I was not going to let this woman get away with this. I knew that I was not making a big deal about this. If I allowed her to speak to me this way, imagine what Tyler had to deal with, I could only think what!

"Janette, you been in this cube all day! Did you even go to lunch? Now it's time to go home, what's up girl?" "Sorry Karry, I was so absorbed with my work today, You know the calls came in fast and furious." I purposely looked down so as to not let Karry, see I was hiding something different on my face. This give me time to act like I was straightening something on my desk. "Well goodnight Janette," "Goodnight Karry." I couldn't get to Tyler quick enough tonight, thank god there was not a great deal of traffic. I rushed to park and get to Tyler. I could hear my own heart pounding in my chest. Wouldn't you know that today the elevators would now come fast enough? As I reached the fourth floor it was all I had to think of was to get to my daughter, As I knocked on the door, I could hear laughing from inside and some of it was Ty's. "Coming, you kids quiet down." I could hear Ms. Karina laughing as she talked to the kids. Apparently they were having lots of fun. "Hi Ms. Rusher, come in Tyler is just about done with her homework." "Mommy, look at me, can we come back tomorrow?" "Sure Tyler, just get yours things." "Ms Karina I can't thank you enough for you taking care of Tyler for me. I love her so much and just want her to be happy." As I spoke I could see Tyler hugging her son, and getting her coat and things. It was great to see her smile, it was so honest and pure. Ms. Karina's son seemed to enjoy her company too. All I saw was two children being kids, why couldn't her school be that way?

As Tyler and I walked down the hall to our apartment, my minded raced back to the problem at hand, although I hid it on my face for the moment. I just wanted to see Tyler's smile and laugh for as long as possible. "Mommy let me open the door, I can reach it please." "Sure Tyler just open the door" it was moments like this that reminded me she was so sweet, something as simple as a door wow, her mind was so innocent she was a simple little girl. What had I thrust my daughter into? I felt so bad many times during this whole ordeal, why must I daily try to justify why I am dealing with this all this crazy crap. What was I going to do next? How dare this teacher Ms. Kent speak to me this way, well I was not going to let her get away with it. Apparently she felt my daughter and I were nobody, and sure I can speak to them any way. I was planning to call the principal in the morning and let her know how ignorant the whole situation was and how I felt hurt and my child. Tyler and I called it a early night, apparently after the incident that morning at school, Ms Kent did not say too much to Tyler that day. Tyler said that the kids were the same, but Ms. Kent did not call on her, or say anything to Ty that day. I asked Tyler how she felt about that, she only responded "mommy it was okay I just tried to ignore the kids being mean to me, I know how you need to work and cannot come to see about me all the time." "Tyler I may have a job, but you are always going to be important to me." As I put Tyler to bed that night I stroked her head and thought about how was this going to play out. Was her teacher now going to just go on as before? Should I just stop going to the school and forget all of this. All I had to do was to look at Tyler and then I knew I was going to make sure she was happy somehow.

I decided to go to work and call back to her school the drive to work that day was uneventful except for my thoughts of Tyler's day. Along with the fact I wondered if Ms. Kent actually thought that I was going to drop the whole incident that happened that morning. Walking into work that morning, it was nothing different from any other morning. My main concern was the fact I was going to make a call to Tyler's principal and talk about her teacher Ms. Kent.

It was not quite so busy this particular day at the job. The calls were going pretty steady, during the lunch I made a call to Tyler's school and apparently the principal had tried to call me, but could not get thru to the voicemail. It seems Ms. Kent wanted to apologize to me about her actions and did not mean to offend me. I left a message for the principal to call me at home. When I got home that day, Tyler again was enjoying her stay with Ms. Karina I saw a happy child when I picked her from her home. Of course when I decided to talk about how her day was going at school, her head immediately fell and she just answered, "Ms. Kent just wants to look mean at me mommy and not call on me

56

anymore." "Tyler just go to your room and put your things away now okay?" "Yes mommy." I decided since it had been days since I answered or even looked at my email I would sit down and take a look. What was so interesting about this particular evening was the fact that I normally don't check my email but every 5 or 6 days. While Tyler was doing her homework and dinner was cooking I decided to check my email. Won't you know it besides the same old advertisement crap, here was a email from Tyler's teacher Ms. Kent. Interesting, Ms. Kent wanted to apologize for according to her the misinterpretation of the way she spoke to Tyler and I. Also she wanted to meet with the principal in the office so the three of us to settle this "problem". I found this so amusing; she decided this as the "problem". Tyler and I ate dinner that night in silence; I only heard the clinging of the plates and silverware. That's not to mention the noise in my head about what was to happen at school next. Each time Ty looked up at me, I just smiled back and told her I loved her.

The next morning after dropping Tyler off I just went directly to work and called the principal's office. I was able to get the principal herself and talk to her about a meeting that same day at lunch. Once arriving at school, I was quickly ushered into the principal's office. It was as if the same "unresponsive ladies" who never wanted to address or look at me, were told to immediately take the time to address me. As I entered the principal's office, I noticed that Ms. Kent was in the office already. Apparently she had given her version of the story of what had occurred in the office. "Come right in Mrs. Rusher, have a seat I do not know what we can do to make it comfortable for Tyler but I would like to get this problem taken care of." Wow that was a lot coming from the principal; I thought she didn't seem to care earlier. Huh, could it be I told her on the phone "I didn't want to see this as a racial issue, which the school could not resolve, and didn't appreciate my daughter being treated so badly." Immediately Ms. Kent stepped up to speak. "Mrs. Rusher I know what happened the other day, but I assure you I want the best for Tyler too. I am so sorry if I offended you in anyway." "Of course you offended me, what do you expect, since you obviously feel that my daughter and I have no right to be here." "Mrs. Rusher, I do not believe that Ms. Kent meant or said something to that fact, perhaps she meant to say did you think about this totally since the percentage of black to white children is small." I looked at both of the woman standing there I only thought one thing, this is going nowhere. "Why can't I have a day at school without any incident, whether it is problems on the playground, or in the classroom? Tyler is made to feel unwanted here, and I don't honestly feel either one you ladies care." "That is not the case Mrs. Rusher, it is about education here. I do know that you want the best for Tyler. "That is correct; I do want the best for Tyler she means everything to me." "Mrs. Rusher, we here at the school just want the best for Tyler as well as all the children here." It was all I could do was to think about Tyler at this point. I quickly excused myself from the ladies in the office as well as a principal and Mrs. Kent I told them that I needed time to think about the situation. As I walked to my car so many emotions was going through my mind, I looked toward the playground I saw children playing I could hear the noise of young children, the voices screaming and laughing, normally this would make me smile back. I could only feel sad and look at the faces of the innocent children and wonder which one was it, that one over there with the pretty curly locks was it that little boy over there. In this same crowd of innocent children are children who were just doing what they had heard or been told to say. It was totally all their fault. As I drove to work, I thought about how some of the simple things we take for granted like watching children play, laughing, talking you don't know there's other things going on there.

Since I decided to take a longer lunch going up to Tyler school, I knew that it would be okay if I took an extra half hour over, being that I had the lady down the hall pick her up today. On the drive home today, I wonder what new development Tyler was going to bring me considering I had a conversation with her teacher earlier this afternoon. Was she going to be evil toward Tyler, was she sorry, I just decided to brace myself and be ready for whatever Tyler was going to tell me this evening over dinner. Turns out nothing bad happened. Tyler told me although she raised her hand, she was not called on in class it was as if she was looked over. So she wasn't picked on since her name was not called and she did know the answer she wouldn't feel foolish. She was just looked over, interesting.

"Mommy can I get the door?" "sure Tyler, go ahead and turn the key. she decided to assist me opening the door." "Mommy I have some homework, to do can I just go get started on it first?" "No problem Ty, I will start dinner." Walking in to the apartment I could feel the different way Tyler walked to her room. It seemed too organized what I mean by that is she seems so focused on going there quickly. I felt Tyler was an average student but tonight for some reason I don't really think that's why she was in a hurry to finish her homework. I could sense something different going on with her right now. Maybe she was thinking about the way she was being ignored from this teacher, did she doubt her own abilities it was so much for her right now. I just knew something else was going on. She was such a blessing to me, it's great when you're an older mom because I needed my patient for her and myself right now. My daughter was miserable and I caused all of this I mean I could've stayed in a different part of town and not got this apartment. I decided to walk toward Tyler's room. She usually rushed out to at least see what was for dinner. As I approached the room she didn't noticed as I peered over her shoulder. There seemed to be a sketch with markers three actual stick people. One person was myself it seemed labeled mom, the other drawing another stick person smaller than the first. And finally the last probably middle dark a lot of marking a weapon of some sort knife. It was actually stabbing the other stick figure much smaller figure marked Tyler. It appeared the knife had pierced the heart area of the smaller figure, there was a lot of red. Blood and more blood, and the blood was coming from the knife. My stick figure was looking over with tears.

"Tyler what is this"? "Mommy ,nothing, nothing mommy nothing." Tyler tried balling up the piece of paper and jam it in the drawer. "No Tyler let me see, stop stop!" Tyler looked up at me I can see she wanted to cry. Softly I spoke, "tell me why Tyler what is this." Of course I knew what it was, somehow her feelings were on this paper in front of me. "Mommy sometimes I dream, sometimes I dream and see I don't belong here. You would be so happy if I was gone from your new apartment." "No Tyler no Tyler this is wrong, I need you we need each other I am so sorry this is what you dream. My world would be shattered if you hurt yourself baby." I lowered myself to my knees to be at eye level with Tyler. "Mommy don't cry, I won't hurt myself."I felt my tears fall down my face, there was so much pain my child felt. I reached out to cup Tyler's cheek and steady hold her directly in front of me. "Please baby believe me, I love you so much. I would not be happy if you were not in my life. Promise me, you will not think about hurting yourself. I will fix this somehow okay." Thru Tyler's tears she nodded. "Please baby say something." "Okay mommy, but what about the dreams mommy, what about them?" I slowly stood up. Tyler's head rose up as if following me for that answer. "Tyler I wish I could say I can stop the dreams. But believe me when I say, I love you and trust me. I tell you what if you have those dreams again let me know. Remember I said God knows and sees everything?" "Yes mommy." Well think about he will not let anything happen to you. Don't forget you remember the

23rd Psalm right?" "Yes mommy." "Whenever you feel sad or unhappy, just recite it to yourself silently okay baby?" "You mean like a whisper mommy?" "Yes angel like a whisper." "It's going to be okay I promise" I hugged Tyler so tight. I could feel Tyler relax close to me, she needed this hug especially tonight."

I was up early the next day, I could not sleep all night I thought about the events. As I looked out over my windows and saw people getting ready for work it must have been about five o'clock. Might as well get breakfast ready for Ty and myself. "Mommy what's for breakfast this morning." "Well let's see Tyler, how did you sleep?" "Mommy are you mad at me about the stick figure in my picture last night." No Tyler, not really I understand you have a lot on your mind right now." "Please forgive mommy, I feel that I let you down Tyler... I'm going to fix this ok. Trust me baby, you deserve to be here just like any other child you deserve to be treated with respect. I could go up to the school in curse and yell and scream Tyler, but that would not solve anything.

I dropped Tyler off the next morning at school and told her to just hang in there. I also told her how much I loved her and wanted her to remain calm, we would get thru this somehow. Tyler looked up at me as she walked to the building, I could tell she still had doubts. I felt it myself. It was so hard to try and concentrate on work that day knowing that my daughter was in so much pain. I did not feel that I was helping her.

Work that day was uneventful, nothing special just the same orders from customers, the phone was very busy that day, I did not get a break hardly to look up from my computer. I decided to just take lunch from my desk and not go out. I felt guilty trying to enjoy my lunch and my daughter was so unhappy.

Janette Ruffin-Rusher

All I knew was that I had to make a decision should I move, which of course was an option. I would of course have to break my lease and there goes my credit. So what, at this point it did not matter, Tyler was miserable. Perhaps I could still stay in Parma but put her in a different school, that would not make a difference to me. I realized that it was still Parma, although I am sure there were people in this city that did not want to cause me harm, I felt that there was also those who want to make life difficult for my daughter and myself.

That night after picking Tyler up, I has so many thoughts to mow over. Tyler had an uneventful day, and she was tired. Ty did share she felt that this was not a happy home and she just wanted to leave. I explained to her that I was still deciding on what to do. I asked her to still believe in me and somehow this was going to change. I shared with her I would like her to just eat her dinner and go to bed, it would be okay, just to trust me. After sitting in Ty's room for awhile watching her sleep, I went back to the living room and decided to read the paper. I remember reading a article in the Metro section of the Plain Dealer and it was from a Regina Brett. She talked about how she felt this man in Cleveland somehow liked to put up racist motivated build boards. Perhaps in his opinion it was not, but the language and the graphic on the build boards suggested something else. What I found so fascinating about this article, is the fact that it seem to speak to me. It talks about, how making statements and inciting violent remarks are hurtful to people. While reading this article, I remember silently tearing up. All I could think of was why do people teach hate, or just care less about who they hurt when it comes to race. This article made me realize this kind of hate would not go away, but there had to be people in this world like Regina Brett who cared and wanted to send a message, just by her column that this is wrong. I was touched by her article, so at the end of the article there was her email address and I sent her a email to thank her for writing. I don't know what I expected to happen, just I felt I wanted someone else out there to know, I appreciated what she wrote and respected her as a writer. I remember writing that I too was dealing with racism and was the single parent of a 10 year old child. I remember saying God bless you and thank you for your efforts.

The next morning, I wrote Ty up at our usual time, and got her breakfast. It was as if the article last night had spoke directly to me. I did not share this with Tyler, I just had a renewed spirit to be strong, and hang in there. "Mommy you seem so happy this morning" "Well Ty I am, you are a great child and it is a shame that some of the knuckleheads at your school don't know it!" "Mommy, knuckleheads?" "I know Ty that is a bit harsh, I guess what I am trying to say is hold your head up high, we are a team and this is going to work out." Tyler looked up from the table and smiled at me, this was a different smile, it was a I believe in you still smile! I could not help but think about how much she looked up to me. I just wanted to make sure she knew I had her back. As I ate my bagel that morning, looking back at her I smiled thru cream cheese teeth, which make her laugh. That was a laugh I longed to hear, she spilled her juice just laughing at me. I knew then it was going to be okay.

At work that next day, all I could think about was the article that I had read. Why did it speak to me so? I was determined to hold my head up high and make sure my daughter was treated fairly. I left her at Ms Karina apartment knowing that there was not going to be any problems that we could not handle together. Work was not as busy today, I watched my voicemail light, so it felt good that no messages had come from my daughter, therefore I thought she must be okay. I decided to take lunch at my desk; I just wanted to concentrate on what my next move was. Should I think about moving, and if I broke the lease would they still charge me for it? Considering what Ty and I was going thru.

"Hello this is Janette," "Ms. Rusher this is the school, and Tyler is having a asthma attack, could you come to the school!!!" Oh my god! I immediately jumped up and went to my supervisor and briefly explained the situation that I needed to go to my daughter's school. On the way there all I could think of was the fact she had her inhaler so why did I need to go? This is not like Tyler not to know what to do. It was hard to concentrate on the road and drive, here she felt that she was not welcome at the school and if she was ill as well, I could only imagine what she was going thru.

Once I reached the school, I went directly to the office. "I am here for Tyler Rusher, I am her mother, where is she?" I was being ushered to a room right off the nurse's office and she was crying still trying to catch her breath. "Could someone please give me her INHALER I YELLED!" Some woman I can only assumed was the nurse handed it to me,. "Here Tyler!" It was all she could do to just pant and pant and try to catch her breath, it looked so sad over and between the tears, I was furious, I was so angry, this was ridiculous! "Tyler should not have had the inhaler in class, Ms. Rusher, because it is medicine, it has to be kept in the office." I looked up at the women speaking and as they say if looks could kill, when she would not have been standing there. "First of all what cause her attack?" "Tyler tried to talk over the tears, but I told her to just relax and I would talk to the teacher. Apparently, a little girl in class had decided to spray some hair spray in the class. Of course she would have to sit right in front of Tyler and the hair spray caused Tyler to have the asthma attack. When Tyler went to get her inhaler from her pocket the teacher Ms. Kent took it upon herself to take the inhaler and tell Tyler it was allowed in class. When Tyler ran out of the classroom trying to get air and breath and get some water. Next she was taken to the office upset and crying and that is where I came in.

"From what I understand, I signed papers at the beginning of the year, where Tyler is allowed to carry her inhaler with her in case of emergencies." At this point the principal steps in to say that no such papers are on file. "I definitely do remember making sure Tyler had such papers on file, just because of her asthma condition." "I am sorry Ms. Rusher that is not the case" "This is a point that I will not argue with you about, the fact is I did and for whatever reason it was lost. Then to add insult to injury, I come here to the school and she is suffering and can't breathe and no one has given her the inhaler!" All the while Tyler was crying and in my lap. She had recovered well enough, but you could see that she was still very upset. It was all I could think to just stay calm. Inside I was burning up and upset, crazy I wanted to scream. I realized just my tone was enough for now and the look I gave conveyed the message I wanted to send. I rose up from the seated position I was in with my daughter I decided to just leave with her in tow. I did not want to get into an argument about what was wrong any more with this situation. I had said enough.

Taking Tyler home, she just laid in the back sit of the car she did not want to talk much. It was enough just to have her home now and safe.

"I feel that you should keep your inhaler in your pocket Tyler. So if you want to take a puff, just raise your hand and say you have to go to the bathroom." "But mommy, won't that be lying about it, if I don't have to go to the bathroom?" "Yes Tyler but it is obvious that we can't trust the teacher Tyler. You are right that it is wrong to lie, but we are going to do what we have to do." "Okay mommy, just raise my hand and ask to go to the bathroom, and then use my inhaler and then go back to class."

"Exactly Tyler, this is where I am asking you to be as strong as you can be right now. You can be right now. You are going to find that sometimes in life you are against the wall and have to stand tall, you understand?" "Mommy I think so." I saw tears in her eyes. I could tell she was just trying to be strong for me. I reached over and hugged Tyler tight. I whispered in her ear. "Baby it will be okay trust, me believe me. God will make it okay. Besides he didn't say it would be easy Angel. I love you too much to let you down, okay Angel. Tyler removed her head from my chest and looked up at me, I could see the start of a smile. "Oh is that a smile Angel? "Yes mommy, I love you." "I love you too." "Okay little lady, lets do this believe me I can't tell you what will happen next. But trust me it will be okay. Tyler and I got to the school early that day. I told the babysitter down the hall that I would take her that morning . As we arrived in the parking lot of the school Tyler and I just sat and talked. I re assured her of my love for her and she must be brave. "But mommy what about how they are treating me here?" "Tyler, you are right, I can see that you will and can see some of the people here are not very welcoming. At least we can see what we are up against. Ignorance Tyler, that is all it is. I am a strong mommy and you are my little angel Ty Ty . So Tyler kill people with kindness. They expect you to be mean, so Tyler still smile. I know it is hard. If they won't play with you. Play by yourself. It will be okay Tyler. Just know that I am proud of you, and it is sad that the kids that are mean to you and have been taught that way. I know that you feel all alone at times right now, is that right Tyler?" "Yes mommy, sometimes I feel that God does not care." "Tyler that is not true, God sees everything that happens. Even what the people here do. Do you still believe God loves you Tyler?" "I don't know mommy." "Tyler the reason I can be strong is because I know God will never for sake me or you. Sometimes God has a plan for what happens and how, but we can not see it always Tyler. I need you to know in your heart even when times seem hard and kids are mean to you, as well as adults. God sees all and I know and believe it will be okay." "Mommy I will try to be nice and don't cry." Tyler's and my eyes both teared up together and then we smiled together. "I loved how just looking at Tyler, it was as if I knew her mind and how she felt at this moment. I hugged Tyler I could see the other children lining up to go in to the school. In the distance children were running and playing. I didn't want to let Tyler go at that moment. I let Tyler and my embrace go, I told her to look through the window. "I know that out there are some great kids like you but sometimes kids just do what they see others kids do. I want you to be my little leader in school today." "What do you mean mommy?" "Well be a leader not a follower, by that stand tall, pretend I am with you and don't follow and be mean like some of the other kids. Show even the mean kids that you are different you understand?" "Yes mommy." "So go and get in line and I will see you later today." "Okay mommy I love you," "I love you too." I kissed Tyler and got a smile. She seemed better for now. I watched her line up and slowly the line disappeared into the school.

The only good thing I could think of was the fact Tyler mentioned early on that she has one friend named Heather that thought that she was nice girl. All I knew about Heather was that she spoke with Tyler everyday and took the time to play with her sometimes I also knew Heather thought Tyler was nice and stood up to the other kids who told her not to play with Tyler. Going to work during all of this was hard for me. I could forget concentrating on work my mind always floated back to my daughter. I felt so alone while I was going thru all of this. My family felt that I should have known better and not moved over here to Parma, my friends said you are on your own. The day at work went slow and dragged just as my thought would constantly go back to Tyler. How was the teacher treating her? I decided to let the negative thoughts just leave my mind for now. The baby sitter picked her up and I would want to hear what she said later. Why take Tyler out of her routine of playing with the other child who played with her at Ms. Karina's house. I wanted to show some type of normalcy. That night when I picked up Tyler I didn't notice anything abnormal or different about Tyler. Just the same she was sad no really jolly or happy, basically going thru the motions. At dinner I asked Tyler about her day and she shared with me that the cross I gave her to wear , a child ripped off her neck and throw it in the sand. Tyler said that she tried to retrieve the cross but the other kids help hid it in the sand and she could not find it. While telling me this story Tyler broke down and said the was sorry she could not find it. She shared with me that her friend Heather tried to help her but she could not find it. Tyler was sobbing and crying As I paced the living room, I wondered what to do next looking out the window of my apartment, I just stared so hard at this point. It was all I could do to constantly tell her it would be okay as I clutched Tyler close to me. I was numb at this point. I took Tyler into her room as she fell asleep in my lap. As I paced the living room, I wondered what to do next. Looking out the window of my apartment, I just stared at the lights in the distance thru flooded tears in my eyes. I decided to just read the paper maybe there was good news to read to take my mind off Tyler and my problems. I could hear silently in the dark Tyler's soft snoring the apartment was silent but except for me clicking the keys on the computer sending the emails. The next morning Tyler awake and I reminded her about the article the other day in the paper. I thought maybe it would make a difference in her mood on her way to school today. "Mommy this lady wants to help us? mommy, do you think she will care about what you said?" "Tyler I just wanted to tell her about us?" "Tyler I just wanted to tell her about us and our story. Tyler it is about being strong and knowing others are out there and feel the same way. Whether or not you know them or not.

Work was uneventful that day. My thoughts went to Tyler and the fact that I should move from here. I could only hope her day was okay. I picked her up from the lady down the hall and all she said was "Mommy cant we leave here, they just don't like us." "Tyler it is not that easy, I have signed a lease with the apartment building and all of our money is gone sweetie I had saved." "So mommy we have to stay here now?" "No Ty I will figure something out." "While eating dinner that night I just wanted to concentrate on having Tyler here with me safe. I didn't want to think about anything else right now. Just my child being safe. I looked over Tyler doing her homework, I realized I was going to have to do something. I didn't know if it meant my job, or break the lease or what but I had to somehow make this better. This was taking a toll on Tyler, she was only ten years old. Our conversations should have been at night about her new friends, and what she learned in class. From the papers she brought home all I could see was failing grades. I knew this was because due to part of what she was going thru.

Little did I know my answer would come in a week, after coming home one evening with Tyler. I checked my email late at night most evening, but it had been a few days with everything going on. So after putting Tyler to bed and laying out her clothes, I noticed I had an email from Regina Brett at the Plain Dealer acknowledging my email. It went on to say that she was interested in interviewing me, and should call her as soon as possible. As I stared down at the email emotions flooded back to me. I thought should I talk to her? What would Tyler think, should I let her talk to Tyler? I decided to just rest on this one. I could speak to Tyler about this later.

Morning came soon enough, while fixing Tyler's breakfast I contemplated if I should discuss this or not. "Good morning Angel." "Good morning mommy." "How did you sleep?""Fine mommy." Tyler seemed n a happy mood, I thought this would be a good time for me to talk to her about the email. "Tyler pass me the juice." "Oh mommy pancakes, yeah." "You seen in a good mood lady." "Mommy I think that it s a good thing that you want to tell people about us." "Why is that Tyler?" "Because it shows we care too mommy, like the lady." "Tyler it is interesting you bring this up, I got a email from this lady at the Newspaper, she wants to talk to us." "What about mommy?" "Well Tyler she wants to interview us both about what is going on at your school." "Let's do it mommy and then we can tell other people." "Tyler you don't understand, once you go to the newspapers, people dig in your business, make up things , its crazy. I'm concerned about you Ty, I am pretty strong and I can take it. On the other hand what about you?" "Well what do you mean mommy?" "Well Tyler, people sometimes may question you, and say you are lying." "Mommy why would people do that?" "Because Tyler that is just how some people are. Tyler do you really think I should do this?" "I think so mommy we have to tell, you told me to be strong. Maybe we can help people with the bad kids?" "You have a point Tyler, I think I will call this lady and maybe we will both talk to her, okay? How do you feel about that Ty?" "Okay mommy if you think it will help us, we should do it." "Ok Tyler, now understand this if you change your mind I will understand." "No mommy, maybe we can help other kids the same way." "How do you mean Tyler?" "Mommy didn't you say god sees everything we do?" "Yes Tyler" "I think that god would like that we are trying to let people know about this and help others." "Tyler since you put it that way I think we will do it then. I will call her back, the lady at the Plain Dealer and arrange for us to meet.

Tyler seemed excited and content for now, I don't know if , she understood the full extent of what was to happen next. One thing for sure, Tyler and I were getting ready for the unknown at this point.

As I dropped Tyler off down the hall at Ms. Karina's apartment I wondered still had I done the right thing. Was I opening up my daughter for ridicule, or perhaps myself. I had to remember this was all for my daughter and maybe by getting her story out if would help others.

Work was the same just a great deal of calls regarding sales and products. I loved my job and speaking with the many different types of customers. I also felt that I had no right to be happy at work when my daughter was so miserable at school. As I took calls throughout my day I found myself constantly glancing at her picture. I tried to think of what strength she was showing, but I also knew she was still wounded her soul was losing its innocence. "Hey lady you don't meet anymore when it comes to breaks Huh?" "No Karry have been so busy with Ty and all." "Yeah right Janette, I know you have been avoiding me when it comes to Tyler and your problems." "Well you want to know the truth Karry, you are right. I felt that you are judging me and really don't feel any of what my daughter is saying is true." "Well actually Janette I thought that was the case." I could see on Karry's face how truly she felt although she smiled. "Tell you what Karry so that we can remain friends let's not talk about it. You have been a friend to me in the past, and for now let's just curtail the subject." I looked up at Karry with the same fake smile she flashed I knew she didn't believe me. "Oh Janette let me get back over to my cube, my break is just about over." I could see she really didn't care about my situation. Although she meant well she was more concerned with how this was going to affect her "city" she grew up in , not my child's welfare. I decided that I was going to do what was best for me and my child. Tyler needed me and I could not be concerned with what others may be thinking.

We talked for hours on the phone, when actually it was about 2 hours. Regina Brett is her name she listened and I felt she did care about racism and ignorance. I had arranged a meeting with her, she then interviewed each us separately. Tyler was shy at first and did not immediately open up to Mrs. Brett. We talked and she listened and asked questions and I could feel she was very compassionate to Tyler. Tyler sipped on the soft drink in front of her. After talking we both just, sat in quiet. "I can tell your daughter is still n a lot of pain." "Yes, but I love her so much and want her to just be happy." "I would like to run your story as soon as possible."

"I felt this is a story I needed to tell, people in this city need to know this was going on. I am sure people in this city are aware maybe they just don't care. I mean we are about to go to war at this time and it's unfortunate this is an issue that will not go away. I moved into a new neighborhood expecting my daughter to have new friends and be happy. Unfortunately so much that has happened is not what we expected." Mrs. Brett went on to say that she was interested in running this story as soon as possible. "That's good and all, but since my daughter is still being taught at school now. I really would like to move first, because if you run this story right away, I am afraid that's kids may still attack Tyler and make her life miserable." Mrs. Brett acknowledged that I had a point and she agreed with the fact I wanted to move first. I went on to explain I needed to break my lease. "Ms. Rusher are you sure this is something you want to do?" "Yes but let me move first." We ended our meet and took the next steps to try and break the lease with no repercussions. Of course I had to find a place to live first.

The ride home was very thought provoking. Tyler asked lots of questions. She wanted to know if the kids would be nice to her once the story came out in the paper. While Tyler was asking me so many questions, I was just trying to get my head around the fact because of this interview I just knew our lives would change somewhat. I glanced over at Tyler and she was just looking the window. I wondered what I had done, did I have her falsely think that now everything was going to be okay.

At home I wanted to just concentrate on what the next step would be. I mainly told Tyler to try and hang in there because I was going to make the next step of getting Tyler and I moved as soon as possible. Sure we still had those days of Tyler being unhappy and sad. Along with the fact I tried to make her comfortable the best way I knew how. Yeah some days were better than others. What I mean by that is less crying or feeling sad, and trying to keep Tyler focused on the fact things were going to get better. So there were days mixed with tears as well as hugs. I worked in a haze many days. I would say it was about 2 weeks from when I did the interview to getting ready to move. I really started to notice Tyler's demeanor was sad and quiet. Yes she was up for a while, but then there were days she would just go thru the motions. "It was okay today mommy." When I knew when I looked at her she was trying to pacify me. I knew my credit was going to suffer I did not care, I decided to break my lease and try to move as quickly as possible. It did not take nearly as long as I thought it would to find an apartment. It was all about who was willing to overlook the fact I had bad credit. Now here I was moving again in less than 6 months.

"Mommy can I open the door, I got the key." "Okay Tyler guess what I have some great news today." As we both walked in from a long day. I knew Tyler needed something to uplift her spirits. "I thought a lot about it and we need to think about moving okay. I have been looking at the fact that what we need to both focus on Tyler is a new start. What do you think Ty?" Tyler looked back while walking to her room. "Mommy do we have the money to move?" "Tyler don't I always make it work?" "Yeah you do mommy." "So don't worry about it, I will be making sure we can move as soon as possible." That night we both slept okay. I knew this would be the beginning of some shorter nights in this apartment. Getting Tyler together in the morning for school did not take nearly as long. I mean she was easy to get ready. It seemed like we both were preoccupied with the fact we were moving soon. "Tyler have a great day baby." She just had to blow me a kiss once last time as we both departed. Standing by the elevator I appreciated knowing while she was in this neighbors apartment, she was going to be fine. Now it was all about getting out of this apartment and moving. It seemed like everything was on auto pilot. First there was an opening in an apartment in Warrensville Hts, Ohio. I knew it was predominately black and although I believed in diversity in school. I was just trying to get Tyler somewhere safe.

Moving Day

"Tyler it is going to be okay, trust me, just hold your head up baby. This is going to be the last time we walk into this school Tyler." I paused with Tyler as we slowly grabbed each other's hands to go into the school and get her transfer. Tyler looked up at me, and forced a smile I grasped her hand so tight. I wanted to assure her by my grip I was there for her. "Mommy is this the last time for us to be here?" "Yes Tyler, it is you have nothing to be ashamed of so walk tall like mommy baby." I made sure I had all my paperwork in order, the new apartment address, the lease signed and her infro from her new school. I was sure they were not going to be ready. I didn't want to get the "oh you have to come back routine." I decided it was NOW.

As we walked in, the office ladies looked surprised. It was that look of what does she want now? As I approached one of the ladies with Tyler in tow, she purposely turned her back to me. I guest this was her way of telling me she didn't want to be bothered. EXCUSE ME I NEED A TRANSFER PLEASE.

Who do I see about it........." It took everything in me to not get louder. I immediately repeated to the lady who turned her back. "I would like a transfer please." She could not help but turn around this time because she had me tap her on the shoulder. "Oh I sorry, can I help you miss?" I knew she knew my name, God knows I had been in this office so many times. "Yes I would like a transfer please, here is my new address and Tyler's new school address. Would I be able to get that today?" At this point the other ladies in the office perked up and I could tell they were really interested now! "Well I believe you will have to wait," "Excuse me I would like that as soon as possible. Can I see the principal, who do I need to talk to in order to get it?" Tyler tensed up next to me, I could feel she was afraid, her fear came through to me. "One moment please Miss...?" "Rusher, Ms. Rusher." I said firmly, the woman immediately stood up and went to the principal's office and shut the door. She was out shortly, I could not see or hear what happen. All I knew is I had my transfer within minutes. "I would like to get her things out of her desk please, is that possible?" Tyler tugged on me, I knew she was afraid I was going to make her go up stairs alone. "Its okay Ty, we will get your things together." "Well I can go up and get her things out of her desk Ms. Rusher." "No, I will go with you along with Tyler. I think it would be a good idea you join us both. So as there would be no delays or problems." I wanted to make it perfectly clear, this is the way it was going to be handled. As I turned to go up stairs, the woman tried to climb them faster than me, it was kinda funny it was as if she wanted to warn the teacher. Tyler and I reached the classroom. I could see the lady from the office inside talking about us. The next thing I knew Tyler's desk was being moved outside to where we were standing. Was I seeing what I actually saw? The teacher did not want us in the class is what I was told by the lady from the office. So that is why her desk was now in the hall for us to clean out. Tyler's teacher did not dare look in my direction, she had two little boys move her desk to the hall and then shut her door. I gathered Tyler's name tag off of her desk and removed all of her things to put in a paper bag I had brought with me. What was so funny was I could feel the tension around us. I don't know if the lady from the office thought I was going to make a scene or what. I am sure I surprised her with my actions. I was just happy to get Tyler's things. Yes deep down inside of me, there was this feeling of wanting to let Tyler's teacher know I didn't appreciate her ignorance. But as this time and place it was not necessary. "Ok Tyler." I loudly spoke. "I think that we are ready sweetheart!" The hall monitor or should I say the office lady looked surprised. There were just the sounds of both my Tyler's feet and mine going down the stairs, and out the building to the car. I knew this was soon to be over. I could feel the eyes on our backs as we left the building.

"Tyler hold your head up baby, you have nothing to be ashamed of. I love you very much." Tyler looked up at me and our eyes met. I could see she felt safe again for now. She grasped my hand even tighter but this time she knew she was safe. That Friday I had requested off and just went home to spend the rest of the day with Ty. We played games, she laughed it was great. I could not wait to move. As I watched Tyler pack up her dolls and put her things in boxes. I felt although she seemed okay, just in her face. I wondered would this last.

Sunday was moving day. I was able to get several friends ready to help. Tyler was to start in her new school in Warrensville, that coming Wednesday. Although I had not been on my job long, I was able to request a few days off. Tyler and I needed time to unpack and I also needed time to reconnect with Tyler. Even though she seemed happy, underneath I could see she felt somehow this was her fault. I knew my child, this again was Tyler just going thru the motions. I tried to make her laugh all day. Whether it was me trying to pick up something that was obviously too heavy for me, just to make her laugh. Or stopping in the middle up moving, to yell out loud hand raised. "I am too old for this Ty." To which I always got the reply, "oh mommy you are never too old." Tyler always tried to make it seem like her mommy always had all the energy in the world. It was very emotional that day, just because I was eager to get this move done. The loading of the truck took forever. Actually all day, I made sure I rented the largest truck I could get so this was going to be one trip. On one of the trips from the apartment down the hall to the elevator, the little old lady down the hall looked so sad. Ms. Hattie had been so kind each and every time she saw us in passing. She was a sweet elderly lady, that always spoke with Tyler and myself. She asked me why I was moving, to which I replied how hard it was for Tyler and I. I remember the look on her fact of shame, I am sure it was not for me. This look I saw on her face was for what she knew we had to endure. This was a very kind white woman of perhaps late 70's or so. Her face was sweet and caring and she said take care of Tyler, I will miss you both. I gave her a hug and said I would. When Tyler and I, along with our friends had unloaded the truck, I remember that Sunday December as a very cold and bitter day. The last load was the hardest, I paused with my hand in Ty's as I locked the door for the last time.

"Mommy it's okay if I don't have anything for Christmas this year. I just want to be with you okay?" Tyler and I sat late Sunday night reviewing the box of mess before us, it was all I could do not to cry. Tyler was hugged up close to me on the sofa. "Tyler I love you, and will do all I can to make sure next Christmas is better I'm sorry we couldn't buy gifts this year Ty." This school will be all better Tyler I promise.

Wednesday morning my main concern was to just get Tyler registered successfully in school. I remember Tyler looking hesitate in her blue and white outfit. The dress code at this school was navy skirts and white blouses. Or a parent could change up with navy slacks or yellow shirts. The only good that that I could at least relax about was the fact the dress code was basic. This worked out fine considering my funds were low.

The principal seemed nice enough and I remember saying what Tyler had been thru. I made the point of telling the principal that Tyler was dealing with a lot of emotions and could he just be patient with her. All I wanted was for Tyler at this time to just fit in. The principal whom was black assured me he understood and he would make her as comfortable as possible. I shared Tyler was scheduled to see a child psychologist to help her get thru her issues. "Could you please make sure that no teachers or kids ask her about the experience in Parma?" I shared about the newspaper article to come along with the fact I didn't want any teachers addressing Tyler about this either. To this I was advised my child would be handled only in the most professional way. Basically I felt that no one should talk to Tyler about her experience after all she was only 10 years old. This I found not to be the case later.

"Tyler give mommy a kiss, you will be fine okay." Tyler walked slowly over to me. She held her breath it seemed. I just wanted to get her to feel secure. I was in such a rush to get her outfit on. Getting her ready, doing her hair that I forgot to look at her face. Here before me stood Tyler with a strange scared look on her face. I only wished I could remain the entire day with her, but I knew this was not possible. One thing for sure, I know my Tyler just wanted friends, that's all. "Tyler you okay honey?" "Yes mommy." I didn't believe her but I kissed her and bent down to look directly in her eyes to say it again. "Tyler it would be okay. I love you see you later sweetie." I got a smile as I rose up, and then Tyler hugged my waist. "I love you too mommy."

This day walking to my car my thoughts were everywhere. Tylers's new school, …was she going to be okay? Would this child psychologist be able to help Tyler. I could see the hurt and also the anger when I looked at her. Any mother knows when their child is in pain and Tyler was still in pain. Rushing to get to work I had to really make time. I trusted that God would take care of everything. She'll be okay, she will be okay, that is all I could think of and keep telling myself. After all here she was in a predominately all black school. Sure I would have loved for Tyler to be happy in a diverse environment but, I thought at least there is nothing that can hurt her now.

Finally I arrived at work only to realize this is indeed the day the article is coming out. I was in such a huff didn't turn on the radio. Apparently some station was discussing the woman in the metro section article about her child in Parma.

As I took the elevator to the second floor. There was certain way the office sounded. Normally you would hear the talk of calls in que, or the quote prices for the items sold. Let's not forget I work in an electronic supply company and there is always a hustle of calls to take and orders to fill. Walking to my cube, immediately I noticed the sudden change of the conversation. Everyone was looking at me with this look of seeing something different or strange about me. You would think I would have picked up what was happening. As I logged in and got my headset on for a minute I thought I was late. "Janette I didn't know you were having problems with your daughter." To my left and standing near me was a co-worker of mind. I really didn't know her name. She was a young woman that had a cube on the other side of the office. "Ah yeah, thank you." Just that quick she disappeared I could see that this was going to be a different and interesting day for me. Around the office I could hear small conversations going on around me. As I put on my headset, my thoughts went to Tyler. I was concerned how her day was going. My phone lines lite up and I started to take calls and fill orders. "Janette can you step into my office for a moment?" I looked up and saw a manager, I worked for asking me to come and speak with him. "Sure no problem." I slowly removed my headset, and I thought I was getting fired. I walked behind the manager to a conference room. I couldn't help but noticed the others in the office having their own side conversations about me. Some of them even had the newspaper article reading it and pointing at me, just in case those in the office didn't know who I was. "Have a seat Janette." I sat directly across from my manager. Joe was a decent person, yes he was white, I would say maybe 36 or 37 but a fair decent manager. Each time I would ask him to leave on short notice to go to my daughter's previous school she just left, he had no problem with it. He never asked why, he would just say it was okay and hurry back soon. I think one of the reasons there was never any problem is the fact I was always on top of my orders. I could only guess what he was going to say. "Janette why didn't you let me know, that you were having problems with your daughter in school of this magnitude?" "Well the times when you would allow me to leave early, or abruptly to go to her school, I was trying to smooth some of these crazy issues over. I mean I appreciate that although I have not been here long you would always be kind and let me go. "Janette I applaud you for taking up for your child. No child should have to feel unwelcome or unhappy in school." "Thank you for that Mr. Clark, do I have to worry about getting fired? I mean I did mention the company that I work for by name and all in the newspaper article." "No you do not Janette, if there is anything I can do just let me know." "Thank you Mr. Clark." With that I went back to my cube. As I walked out of the conference room, the employees around me scattered. I could see they were searching my face as well as my manager to see if I was fired. Or maybe crying, or something. Yes there was still tension there, but I just wanted to work and for a minute wondered if I had done the right thing. Just for a moment, I second guessed myself, Yes I did Tyler was right people needed to know her story. I could not wait to get home from work and greet Tyler. In this new chapter I was smart to arrange for Tyler to attend a daycare. Tyler was admitted with no problem, and I felt that she would be fine. The afterschool program she was enrolled in actually had kids of all ages. So she could feel free to interact and make some new friends. It was nice to hear children laughing and playing. Tyler I noticed was talking with a couple of girls her own age. "Mommy I didn't hear you come." "Hey Ty, had fun today?" "It was okay mommy." I gathered Tyler's hand to move over to the front desk to check Tyler out. "Somebody made some friends today, huh." The lady sitting at the front was nice and polite, she told me about how Tyler mainly was quiet right after school getting there. Later she said Tyler opened up and started to play with the others. I shared a little about Tyler's previous school and she may need time to adjust. "Tyler did great today, Ms. Rusher." "Thank you, we'll see you tomorrow. Tyler and I still had boxes to clear and put away. She really did not share much about her new school at first. Then while putting things away she just started to open up. "Mommy some of the kids just stared at me today." "Well Tyler did you try to make some new friends?" "I just was quiet because some of the kids mad fun of me." This is all I needed at this time I thought. Calm down, I thought to myself. You are seeing something that is not there. "What do you mean Tyler." "A teacher asked me was I the girl in the paper." My back was faced in front of Tyler, while I washed dishes. The was good considering I am sure on my face I soon showed how I was pretty upset. As I turned around I saw Tyler was finishing her milk. "So Tyler tell mommy what the teacher said again honey." "Well mommy I told the teacher, that I could not talk about it. That you my mommy told me not to." "You did correct Tyler, I will take care of it. Do not talk about any of what is happening in Parma. Let mommy take care of it." Tyler and I put more things away. Putting the dishes away together was strange. "Mommy do you think we will have a Christmas tree this year? "Tyler I will see if I can make that happen." There was no way we were going to be able to get everything put away tonight. Tyler's bed is what was important first. Tyler went to sleep fast. I figured it was her busy and fast day. I didn't want to harp on the newspaper article with what may or may not happen at school.

"Tyler get up honey." Tyler was already in the bathroom as I approached her room. Maybe a good sign, she was eager to go to school. "Mommy can I wear one of my new shirts?" Tyler had several new blouses, all dress code but the pale blue I knew was her favorite. Tyler favorite color was blue. I prepared Tyler's breakfast along with her asthma medicine. Tyler was diagnosed with asthma since she was 3 and I just learned to manage it with her as best I could. "Got your inhaler Tyler?" "Yes mommy, right here." "Here watch television sweetie." I took Tyler to her school the first day, Today I was going to walk out to the bus stop with Tyler and wait. Once outside I could see how far the stop was from our apartment. Tyler had problems walking in the cold with her asthma, I knew this was not something I wanted to deal with. Looking out the window I could see it was windy and cold. I decided I would have to definitely figure something out. Tyler could not walk in this regularly with her asthma. It seemed that although I stayed on top of Tyler's meds she still had problems with the cold air. I found myself plenty of times making sure she took a treatment on her nebulizer. After bundleing Tyler up she and I strode slowly to the bus stop. I would say we waited about 20 minutes until the bus showed up. I told Tyler to sit near the front of the bus, and everything would be fine. For some reason I assume the bus would have only kids of her age, that was not the case. As the bus pulled up, there was no order all the big kids push the little kids out of the way and it was chaos. Although it bothered me how rude the kids could be. I just waited till the end of the line with

Tyler and she got on. There was one other parent out there, she spoke hello briefly and rushed back to her apartment. I watched the bus turn the corner at the light toward the school. Bitter cold never agreed with me, I was just glad Tyler was dressed warm.

Work had the atmosphere of strangeness as I arrived. I looked around the office as I walked to my desk and people seemed to not want to look at me, What was I the plague now. Even my manager that was so nice, seemed to look down when he looked in my direction. There was a strange feel around me. As I walked from the copier to my desk with some paperwork that I needed, I saw people avert their eyes away from me if I looked in their direction. Was the reason for this the newspaper article? I felt the coldness in the office toward me. I found out later some of the managers and others employees resented me talking about my problem with my child. Of course I did mention the name of the company I worked for. So apparently that did not go over with some of the employees. I was never a clique person so it was okay for me to remain alone. I always ate lunch alone, except with my friend Karry. Not that I was anti social, just pretty much a person who kept to herself. Everyone before this article in the office did speak to me. Now everyone acted as if they were told not to look or talk to me at all, unless it was job related. I worked thru my day, I saw the stares and the side conversations. I decided to just concentrate on Tyler and how her second day must be going. I wanted to just get thru this and back to normal as soon as I could If I could.

Driving to pick up Tyler I found it hard to believe what I had endured in less than 6 months. Moved twice and enrolled Tyler in 2 different school systems. How was this taking a toll on Tyler, considering she was schedule to start seeing a child psychologist this week as well. I mentioned to Tyler that I felt she needed to talk to someone, other than her mother. Tyler thought it was silly and not necessary to talk to any doctor is how she put it. Walking in I could hear the children laughing and talking. I walked in and saw Tyler off in the corner to herself. This was something, I guess I knew was there all along, she was just trying to be invisible I saw and to herself. "Hey baby why are you sitting there ? You ready to go Ty?"Tyler rose slowly gettings her things. "Sorry mommy, can we just go home." "Yeah Ty, what"s wrong, you not having fun here?" "No mommy it is okay, the kids are okay." We walked to the front desk for check out. When I signed Tyler out, she walked pretty quickly to the car with purpose. "Tyler wait up honey, I am on my way." Unlocking the car, Tyler couldn't get in quick enough. "Hey lady how was your day?" "Mommy some of the kids at school say she think I am strange and weird. At gym they laugh at me and says things about what their parents said about me." "What do you mean Tyler?" "They say I smell bad like the paper said, and that you are not a good mother. One kid said you just wanted attention that is what his mother said about you. These kids don't want to be my friend mommy. They don't like me!" After that last outburst, Tyler hung her head and started to cry uncontrollable. Just about the time I parked the car outside our new apartment. I stared forward looking up at the second floor baloney of where we lived. Was I froze what to say now? Stepping out the car I immediately opened the back door to help Tyler out with her book bag. "Tyler let me wipe your face, no tears in the cold baby. Come on lets go in the apartment. Tyler and I walked into the apartment with my arms around her. "Sit down Ty, did any teachers intervene when kids were mean to you?" "No mommy, they just looked, like they were waiting for me to do something. Or they would just tell the kids to be quiet." Great I thought now I have to try and deal with another set of ignorant behavior. As I looked at Tyler, I saw a more changed child. I mean I could see pain on her face as she looked forward. I wondered what she was thinking at this point. Did she feel I had put her in a more hellish situation? Did she feel so betrayed by me and how maybe this was her fault. Just looking at Tyler, I didn't understand why all this was happening to us. Here it was a couple of weeks before Christmas and ironically it was nothing going on around me to feel like it was Christmas. Tyler throughout this never once has asked me for any toys she just wanted to go to school and have friends. Tyler did wait for me to give her some type of response. She had walked back to her bedroom filled with boxes and sat on the bed. What to say I thought as I entered the room. "Mommy why is this happening to me?" "Tyler I really don't know. Some people out here are just mean. I will go to the school in the morning and talk to the principal, okay?" "Mommy are you mad at me?" "No Ty, I just feel so bad that you have to go thru all of this. One thing I want you to know is that, it is not you. Some kids are just cruel, but please trust me Tyler. I will try to make this right. I love you very much. We have an appointment tomorrow night with the doctor Ty, and I want you to not be afraid?" "Mommy what type of doctor is she?" "Well she talks to children and try to help them deal with issues. I mean she tries to help children feel okay about their feelings. This lady Tyler is going to ask you all types of questions and that might seem to be too personal. You understand?" Tyler looked up at me and I could see she was searching for something to say. "Mommy I think that if you say this will help, I will do it okay?" I hugged Tyler, this was going to be a path to something. I was not sure yet. I just knew I had to get Tyler help. She had made a change, and I could see it. Tyler's tone was monotone since the move. Sure it was just a few days, but the whole thing had changed Tyler, she was definitely different.

The next morning I had a great deal to do. Tyler needed help and tonight hopefully will start that help. "Tyler don't let that water constantly run in the sink Ty?" "Okay mommy, I am almost done brushing my teeth. I didn't want to be late getting to school in the morning and talking to the principal. This was so stupid what I was dealing with, but then again this was elementary school. She just needed to make an adjustment as a new student. This is what I wanted to believe.

When we go to the school, it was so disorganized, I mean children people running in all opposite directions. The office was so loud phones ringing, kids trying to talk, just loud. "Excuse me, excuse me I need to talk to the principal please. Pardon can I speak with the principal please?" Finally a woman stopped what she was doing at her desk and looked up. "Yes, can I help you?" "This is my daughter Tyler, I would like to see the principal please." "May I ask what this is about?" Being that it was so loud in the office, I didn't want to yell out what I wanted. "I would prefer to speak with the principal direct if I could please." I changed my tone to sound more firm, I really rather not discuss this right now." "Okay have a seat right there, and I will get someone to help you." I found a seat over to the side." Looking around the office all I saw was chaos, this told me right away that this was not a good vibe. Little did I know I was only so right. "Can I help you please?" I looked up and there was the principal in front of me. "Ms. Rusher can I help you, step over to my office. "I walked down the hall to his office thru the chaos in the hall. Tyler clung very close to me and I noticed not a single child smiled at her.

"I am so sorry Ms. Rusher, it apparently has been an adjustment for Tyler and I think it is going to take some time. "Well you and I both know that this is true of new kids to any school, but I feel some of the things that she is telling me should not be happening." As the principal spoke to me I could see he was preoccupied with all of the noise outside of his office. It was difficult to hear with all that was going on. Kids screaming, no organization, parents yelling. All I could think of was what the hell had I put Tyler in now.

This fifth grade year was pure horror for Tyler, it seemed like everyday Tyler came home crying upset and had to fight back to kids picking on her. During this time I tried desperately to calm her fears and work with her by having her go to the child psychologist twice a week for 6 months straight. This along with the collage I created in Tyler's room to help her better about herself and her color. You see Tyler was already uncomfortable with her dark skin from the incidents in Parma and now she just was worse due to the fact she still had problems. She could not understand why kids that looked like her picked on her and the authorities in charge did nothing or blamed it on her and said she wanted attention. How did I deal with it? Well not good at all, I always had to go up to the school and either verbally had to go off about the bullies, and when Tyler reacted back with violence she was told she had mental problems by the kids and teachers alike. I felt like because I brought attention to her once with the article, now I was being punished more for it. No to mention Tyler had a jewish woman for a child psychologist and she did not like it at first. My reasoning was that I wanted Tyler to see that not all white people were mean and cruel. That there was ignorance in all races, and that it was about finding a doctor that could address Tyler's issues. I didn't want her to grow up with hate. I wanted to help her, and felt if I showed her that she could move pass the pain it would get better. It was hard doing this since the new school that she was in was not a happy experience for her at all. Sure there were 2 or 3 kids that were friends to Tyler but overall she was so unhappy. I decorated her room with pictures of all the different shades of black people. Pictures of black people both famous and not. Everyday people, that I had cut out of magazines, and each one was pasted around her face.

Fifth grade turned out to be just hell for Tyler, her asthma got worse and she because one unhappy child. A great deal of what she had to deal with was the fact no teachers made her feel like they cared. No I must correct that, one teacher by the name of Mrs. Summers made Tyler smile. From what Tyler told me about her, she tried to make the kids stop teasing Tyler or picking on her. The fifth grade year was hell for both Tyler and myself. I was trying to make the adjustment for Tyler as well as go back to normal at work. Around it was the constant buzz of who does she think she is to talk about a city. Or I would overhear people talk about why does Janette always have to leave and go home early. Many times I left because I had to go to the school in Warrensville because Tyler was involved with another altercation with another student. Fights fights and more fights. When we talked at home, Tyler said she did not understand why kids were mean to her. Then we I went to the school, it was confirmed she did not start the fights, the other kids started each and every incident. I felt at times the school was not doing enough to stop the bullying and fights in general with the kids. Because when I did go to the school to get Tyler in anyone of this incidents, there were always others kids in the office with parents and yelling and screaming going on. One occasion I tried to talk to a guidance counselor about how she addressed Tyler, and that did not go well. I ended the meeting very upset with how the counselor was not trying to mediate and work with the kids.

After a couple of months I could see that Tyler was very depressed and just did not like going to school. I thought the child psychologist would help, but only to a point. I mean she was a very qualified professional and Tyler eventually took to her, but there was still an unhappy child there I could see. Tyler because withdraw and angry with the world. She told me she felt that kids hated her because she was not a good person and that it was all her fault. I talked to Tyler regularly about that not being true and that she was special and a good person. She could not see this fact, just due to the fact all the chaos going on around her. I made so many trips to the new school for Tyler fighting, or kids picking on her that I wondered if any learning was going on. I just tried to constantly remind Tyler that I loved her and please open up more to me. Sometimes she did and then there were times she just would not. When I made random visits to the classroom and wanted to stop in and see what was going on, that was a real interesting treat as well. There was always disruption in the classrooms kids not paying attention, kids picking with other kids, and the teacher or teaching to a select group the group trying to listen or hear.

Soon spring was here and the weather broke, I needed some way to make Tyler open up and be a happy child again. I felt that somehow, my little girl was lost inside what was just the shell called Tyler Rusher. Looking into her eyes each and everyday getting her ready for school she was just going thru the motions. Tyler told me she hated school and hated how she always had to fight and defend herself. Each and everytime I spoke with the principal about these incidents, he would say I will address them and the parents. But of course things just continued. Somehow one day a teacher overhear Tyler singing to her self in a classroom one day and she told Tyler how well she sounded. Tyler could not wait to tell me about it, it was the first time in a long time I could see the light come back to her eyes. Tyler and I would ofter sing around the apartment and I knew she loved to sing, but to have a teacher in school tell her that made her so happy. Not to mention having even some of the bullies tell her that they liked her voice too, really make her feel accepted. I decided to encourage her even more to sing if asked. Well wouldn't you know luck would have it some of the kids told the principal how Tyler could sing and one day she was asked to sing over the PA system. Something to do with after the announcements were read. Tyler came home so excited and all she could talk about was "mommy they asked me to sing, they ask me to sing over the school PA!" Well we had to find a positive good song, I forgot the occasion, but it had to be an uplifting song. Well I knew the song that would be it. Tyler and I decided on Mariah Carey's song Hero. I had heard Tyler sing that song in her room and loved that she said to me once how I was her hero. The day Tyler said that, I remember asking her how is that Tyler? She said because mommy you never stopped loving me.

That was it the music, I made sure Tyler took her instrument to school and I took the time to talk to the music teacher about Tyler's saxophone and how she could read music. Bam just like that occasionally there was life coming back to Ty's eyes. She loved music and singing, this paved the way for her to meet a new friend by the name of Dajia who was also a girl in music and played a instrument. Sure they had their ups and downs like friends do, but she started to come back a little. Dajia introduced Tyler to a couple other kids who saw Tyler was nice and fun. Sure the 5 grade still was rough but at least she had a couple of friends. The day she came home excited about the fact she sang her song was the best. "Mommy everybody like my song, they said I can sing!" "I know Tyler you have a beautiful voice I am so proud of you." We embraced so much that evening, all she could talk about was the fact that everyone liked her voice. Another day of happiness for Tyler.

I was so glad when the 5th grade was over, Tyler made it thru to the 6th grade. Now that I could see what I was dealing with in the school system. I decided to just concentrate on making sure Tyler had my support and and as much of a positive environment at home as possible. I felt as much as I had to go back and forth up to the Elementary school and address stupid discipline problems, that showed me what I was up against. I felt the administrators had labeled Tyler a bad kid that just wanted attention and mental issues. Sure no one told me this but base on the negative feedback I would get each and every time I had to address an altercation, I knew that was the case. Don't get me wrong I did not want her to fight at all. But how many times can you continually call, and call and ask the principal or teachers to control the bullies and nothing happens and not expect a child to act out their pain. When I would talk to Tyler about her anger or fights with children, she would say sometimes mommy I see the kids from Parma who picked on me and taunted me. I tried many times to express this to the principal and it was met with I feel Tyler just wants attention and doesn't have to fight back all of the time. There were more sessions with the child psychologist and therapist, but I soon realized it was up to me as a parent to talk with my child and work with her for growth. I decided over the summer since Tyler liked to sing so much I would encourage her to sing more. We both decided since I had a friend in Cleveland that worked with summer festivals and talents shows for kids, Tyler could sing with other kids. When I talked to Tyler about how this would help her to feel good about herself and how good she made people feel, she agreed this would be a good idea. Tyler had a self esteem issue with how people treated her. I could see she felt insecure about herself. Tyler was still stuck in that I am so bad and ugly that is why people don't want to be my friend. I had set in my mind I was going to change all of this the best way I knew how.

Over the summer I tried to spend as much time with Tyler as I could. Sure I had to work, but I made sure she was either at her Grandmothers, or daycare. Tyler was 11 years old now and actually I felt old enough to stay at home by herself. But I still felt that just dealing with all the issues still on her plate, it was best she had other kids around or just type of friendly environment. Tyler's uncle had brought her a karaoke machine and she and I would sing all the time on the weekends. It gave her some much joy to sing, that was one of the few times I would see her light up and smile. After all of this singing I decided to enter Tyler into a festival in Cleveland call the annual Glenville festival. We both decided that since she was so good at singing the Mariah Carey song "Hero" she would sing that song.

After that song, there were more summer festivals and I enjoyed seeing this side of Tyler. Sure sometimes she would say things like "I know school will be here soon mommy, right?" What was so strange was the way she would just blurt out this statement or rather question at once. As if she wanted me to respond or just look at her. Most times I would just look over and smile. I could see she knew I was acknowledging her concern. My summer working with Tyler for this next transition was going to be interesting because although I could see the happiness. I also could see a hurt child that was clinging to whatever way she could. I knew Tyler was not quite ready to go back to school. Its interesting that as I dealt with this move ,I somehow knew that this journey was going to be growth for myself as well as Tyler.

The sixth grade year had started and Tyler was not too happy for the first day. Sure we had fun over the summer, but most times she spent it over her Grandparents house while I worked. I did not always leave her at home alone. I know 11 years old is okay. Just concerns over leaving her alone with her thoughts worried me somewhat. Tyler needed interaction with her Grandparents and she especially loved her papa. They had the best relationship. Although I did not have a good relationship with my Dad, I appreciated the fact he adored Tyler. That was I believe in my heart was helping Tyler to heal inside. Regardless of what the new school year had to offer. Tyler and I would get thru it. I knew my daughter needed as much love as I could give and I was not going to let anything damage that part of our lives.

My main concentration in the sixth grade for Tyler was getting her thru her subjects. She seemed to have teachers that were more concerned with all the behavior and fights and she just got lost in the shuffle. Yes she still seemed to have altercations with kids, but now it was as if with every fight she was involved with, kids soon found it fun to pick with the strange kid is what she told me. Why was she considered strange, well lets see. Her wanting to wear her hair in a gel down Mohawk. I didn't have a problem with it, sure I talked to Tyler about the fact kids already wanted to pick with her because she was considered different somehow. On the other hand I always endorsed the fact that she wanted to be different as part of her artistic expression I thought. I was clinging to the fact I didn't want her to feel that I was not supporting the fact she wanted to be different. Whether it was her taste of music now, which included rock, r and b, heavy metal or just pop. We sat down plenty of times and talked about while I was supporting her different tastes in music and hair styles. I wanted her to also realize that when you decide to be different and bring attention to yourself, you have to be willing to also accept the fact there are people waiting and ready to ridicule and pick on you. I knew deep down this was just Tyler's way of expressing her pain. We still talked about the fact regardless of the race, some kids and people in general are just ignorant and mean. This was a hard lesson at times to home in to Tyler sometimes in our talks. She was always trying to rationalize why this was happening all to her. I told her that I could not understand it either, but that she had to talk to me about the pain sometimes and how unhappy she was.

7th was a real treat, Tyler was so nervous going to junior high school. Tyler mentioned to me that she heard the junior high school was all trouble. I asked her all summer, and also advised her. "Tyler relax, I know this is junior high, but Tyler you just do Tyler. I love you and your are a tough strong young lady. Please think about the fact you have gotten thru worse than this."

She went to school that first day and made it. Of course their were the school's share of bullies. The junior high school went from 7th grade to 8th grade. Tyler showed signs of more anger I could see it, she had built up this ruff wall and didn't smile as much anymore. I mean she didn't react any different to me. It's just she really hated the junior high. I got the impression the many times I went to the school that these teachers were just dealing with the bad kids, and you had to just fit in. I hate to say it but there were more fights and more fights. Behavior issues isn't really a good enough word to describe what I felt and saw. Rather a teacher who leaves the room when kids have an altercation screaming. So of course no one saw "anything" is what I was told. Or the fact Tyler is in the office with another child who decided to throw text books at Tyler. Well let's see, he was bored. Of course the teachers already had decided to ignore this child and just go on teaching. So according to Tyler, she took matters into her own hands and throw books back to the point of extreme. No I didn't appreciate that behavior by Tyler either, but she was trying to deal with things the best way she could. I was still allowing Tyler to express herself. So while she was quite an obedient daughter at home with me. I accepted the different tastes in clothes and hair, all while wearing a uniform of black and white to school. Since Tyler could not express herself in changing her outfits, she was allowed to express herself in her hair. Kids resented it and thought she was strange or weird, but again I knew she was acting out her pain. Even in her English class , I saw it in her writing. Tyler point of view on the world I saw had changed even. I encourage her to voice her opinion so she could feel better about herself. This was important to me so I cared a lot about how she felt about self esteem. Tyler needed this armor to help her feel safe and confident again. I was not going to let her for a minute feel sorry for herself. Yes she had experienced racism, and now just pure ignorance. We talked at great length one afternoon I remember about how people and kids in general can be closed minded about things they don't know or understand. This I told her mean't just being able to accept differences was the key. We got thru 7th grade with a lot of tears and hurt, and patience. I am sure it was wrote in her files that she was different, wanted attention or acted out. When I knew she just wanted acceptance and an education. I had been up to Tyler's junior high so many times that year. So no, I was not an absent parent. I believe this is what for lack of a better word, is what pissed off her teachers. Each and every time I went to Tyler's school I wanted answers, I was not going to go away. I know the principal and some of the teachers resented me. Why because I encouraged Tyler to be proud of who she was. Not to be afraid to be different. Of course I didn't want her disrespecting teachers. Which she didn't , but on the other hand I did tell her to speak up and not be afraid to express her opinions. She deserved an education and although this was not in my opinion a good situation. Tyler was going to get thru it.

8th grade was here, over the summer we went to the library more. Tyler enjoyed the library, I told her how you could travel the world thru the library. This I found helped her get her mind off the hurt and the pain she felt inside. Yes it was still there, except she had changed over the years and became deeper inside herself to outsiders. I wanted to have Tyler still feel that she could trust again. When 8th grade started, she was stronger mentally, I could see. But on the outside surface, I knew kids over the years in this system had labeled her as weird and mean. Mean because she stood up for herself and weird because she choose to express herself. Tyler expressed herself in her singing and just trying to have those friends she wanted a few years back. Yes there was still some fights, just due to the fact some kids had to prove themselves to the weird kid. The girl that like rock and Mohawks and talking about how it is okay to be different. Tyler was considered the different kid by her teachers for the most part too. Yeah there were maybe one or two who saw her as a outspoken smart kid. On the other hand she was also told by some teachers, she should try to fit in as well. I had no problem going to the school to support my daughter and insist she be allowed to be different. Her views and that fact she was not conforming with the others was perfectly fine with me. Let's see how was it said to me. "Maybe Tyler would not have so many altercations if she would just be silent and not stand out so much." Which was told to me by one administrator. To whom I responded. "I guess it's okay to pick on a child that wants to be different right." Many times I am sure the teachers and admistrators did not like the fact I made it a point that they knew I was there for Tyler and she was going to progress and make it thru this inspite of them. Sometimes I felt the teachers wanted me to be just like the parents out there that didn't care and never question what was going on in or at their child's school. I personally felt that this system had failed her .

Over the summer Tyler was so happy she had made it thru the 8th grade. I keep reminding her about the fact she did it she was going to be okay. Tyler did not know I had made plans to move again. I didn't want her to take on her high school years in this school system. I am sure she just assumed she was going to the high school. Tyler expressed the fact she hated the fact she had to deal with some of the other trouble makers again in her high school in the fall. I still won't soon forget the look on Tyler's face when I told her we were moving again. "Mommy for real, we are moving oh my god!!!! How, when what!" "Tyler I know how much you hate living here, it is about you, as a mother. I have asked so much of you. To be strong in spite of how some of these kids have treated you. I have endorsed you wanting to be different and have enjoyed it all because I love you. But on the other hand, you deserve to be happy, while getting your education." I remember asking Tyler to sit down. We were sitting in the living room this Saturday afternoon and I remember asking Tyler to turn the television off to hear what

I had to say clearly. "Tyler, you know how you and I always talk about inclusion and accepting people for their differences?" "Yes mommy I do" "Well Tyler we are moving into another community that is diverse and actually the school system is children of all ethnic backgrounds. Now I know what you experienced in the past, you and I both know that. This move will I believe show you a better environment of acceptance Tyler. I just believe this in my heart." "So basically what you are saying is I will be going to a school system with kids white and black?" "Tyler it is not about black and white, it is about diversity and differences and acceptance. I want your high school years to be fun and you feel good about yourself. You do not need to feel that you must fight each day you go to school or have to fight. You will be going to the Orange School district Tyler. I found us an apartment so lady we are out of here!!" Tyler sat silent for a minute and just looked at me. I didn't know what she was thinking at this moment. Then it came, a smile, a big smile. Then a hug for me. "Why didn't you tell me sooner mommy?" "Well Tyler I just wanted to make sure financially everything was in place. I just wanted this to be a smooth transition for the both of us. I know you have endured so much throughout all of this, and I love and want the best for you." Tyler and I hugged for a long time I could feel her heart. She was coming back, some of the pain was leaving her even now.

Summer was great we went swimming and just got ready to move. Now was the time for getting excited about her new school. Tyler had a lot of questions about what if the white kids were mean again and now even older. I assured Tyler that this was not the case. This was a totally enriching environment and she could be who she was. I only knew a little about the Orange School system but I knew each time I looked into the information I could gather it was very good. I wanted so much for this move to make a difference and yes I was nervous. In my gut though I knew I was making the right decision.

Tyler and I received after all the registration paper work , an invite for all new students that were freshman. When we arrived at the school we were welcomed by the principal a Mr. Hanstein. We walked around the school with the other parents and were shown all the areas important to new freshman parents. Tyler saw other kids and noticed how nice and polite, yet sly some were. I could see her somewhat relax. This occurred a couple of days before school was actually in session so there were only freshman and their parents there. I enjoyed the tour myself and felt that I had made the right decision.

"Mommy I am so scared and nervous, what if the kids call me names and want to start things?" "Tyler we have had a great summer, new apartment, new chapter. Relax it will be okay, I know it baby." I faced Tyler and now she stood as tall as I was now. Over the years she had grown tall. Before me stood a young lady that had grown from a little girl. "You are right mommy, I can do this, and I love you." The drive to the school was silent. This I believe not because we were angry or anything. Just we both had thoughts of this big day. When I dropped Tyler off in front of her new school she hesitated at first. Then there was that smile and she went in. At work that day, all I could think of was how is Tyler today. I mean she was not 10 or 11 now, she was 15 and now time had changed her some what. She had a cell phone and I knew she had to grow up. I talked to her about accepting others that morning and now having to solve problems with violence. She agreed to try and think in a positive frame of mind and be excited about high school.

When I got home that day from work, Tyler was only so excited to talk about school. "Mommy I have friends !! Kids were actually nice to me, you were right I love my new school. It seemed so weird at first having kids come up to you and hug you and want to get to know you. I love my new school!! We both had tears in our eyes, I knew we both were thinking the same thing no more pain. Maybe she could just be a regular kid in school. Tyler talked about how accepted she felt and the teachers being welcoming. She talked, and talked and talk.

Since coming to Orange High School, Tyler had never been happier. She is now in the 12th grade at Orange High School I would say has been a ball for her. Tyler became a Lionette, which is a flag girl in the band, Her friends are of all ethnic backgrounds. I love the fact we have been to basketball games and football games and both of us have felt welcome. Tyler was able to be in a play, and let's not forget choir is of course her favorite. I loved listening to her talk about her teachers and how they cared. I saw parents active in their kids lives. I saw this with the different parents regardless of race. Most importantly I wanted Tyler to see the world differently. That people are all not bad and these administrators and teachers did care. Tylers Pain was now gone. Thank you Orange High School.

Tyler and her Powder Puff Dolls

Singing Mariah Carey's Song Hero

Graduation Picture 2010